It's A Jungle Out There

Also, by Nathaniel A. Turner:

Raising Supaman

Stop The Bus: Education Reform in 31 Days

NATHANIEL A. TURNER, JD, MALS

It's A Jungle Out There

Powerful Parenting Lessons Inspired by The Lion King

It's A Jungle Out There Copyright © 2019 by Nathaniel A. Turner, JD, MALS. All rights reserved. Printed in the United States of America. No part of this book may be used or reproduced in any manner whatsoever without written permission except in the case of brief quotations embodied in critical articles and reviews. For information, address Two Crabs and a Lion Publishers, 450 E. 96th Street, Indianapolis, IN 46240

Nathaniel A. Turner, JD, MALS books may be purchased for educational, business, or sales promotional use. For more information, please e-mail the Books Division at nate@nathanielaturner.com.

FIRST EDITION

ISBN 978-0-9895879-0-7

Library of Congress Cataloging-in-Publication Data has been applied for.

Author's Note

The thought of writing a book was once a foreign concept. I have always questioned if anyone would care to hear what I had to say. My mantra for not writing a book was, "Who am I to write a book?" I now hope that after reading this book, you don't ask the same question.

Over the last several months, I have learned that writing a book is a very ego intensive process. No one wants to write a book that others hate or, worse, don't bother to read. I have hoped not to be the proverbial tree in the forest that falls, and no one hears, sees, or misses when it comes tumbling down.

Because my ego is so fragile and its vulnerability would have preferred for me to have discontinued this journey long ago while writing the book, I have reluctantly tried to ignore the image that I have of myself failing spectacularly. Nonetheless, here I am nervously expressing my thoughts and sharing them with the rest of the world or at least with whoever cares to read what I have to say.

I believe this journey is necessary. Convinced by the exceptional people throughout human history who freely shared their truths – many of whom did so even in the face of death, I realize that I should not allow my fragile ego to keep me from accepting my responsibility to do the same.

My life is not in jeopardy, although humanity is at a crossroads. Perhaps humanity has always been at an intersection. Maybe it's just me, and I'm now more compelled to say something because I'm a father. I certainly feel more attuned to the tremors shaking the ground of this Nation and the planet far more than any time previously.

Around me, I continuously hear from politicians, clergy, community leaders, and the like that family is the most essential element of the American fabric, yet families are eroding from sea to shining sea. From our preferential unmindful assimilation of technology to the explosion of online education to the reduction of in-person socialization to the decline in the traditional two-parent household to the normalized proliferation of single parents, America and her families are coming apart at the seams.

In my humble estimation, the deteriorating fabric of our land is an illustration of much more than normal wear and tear. Since its founding, this land – your land and my land – always frayed at the seams has been falling apart faster than ever due in significant part to inadequate and nonexistent parenting.

Many people have children, but only a sprinkling of parents appear to be interested in raising critical thinking, globally competent, humanitarian-oriented citizens.

Smartphones, video games, tablets, computers, nannies, acquisition of stuff, the pursuit of more things, scheduled visitations, school counselors, law enforcement, probation officers, psychiatrists, and coroners have replaced quantifiable and quality family time and purposeful parenting.

Where have all the parents gone? What happened to those who, like my grandmother, treated parenting as the most important human responsibility and the planet's oldest profession? My grandmother, if she were living, would not recognize today's parents.

Something is amiss. We reside in a country that places higher demands on passing a driver's education course than it does on procreation and raising children. We offer classes like Lamaze to prepare parents for the birth of a child but have no such courses to equip parents for being able to raise a child. The way we view parenting and subsequently raise children is absurd.

So, I wrote this book because I believe my grandmother would have wanted me to say something. I wrote this book because I'm concerned that if we wait much longer to outline a process to help our future citizens, we won't be able to repair or recondition the fabric of our nation. I wrote this book because I believe all children need and deserve great parents.

From the review of scenes from *The Lion King*, we'll explore parenting themes that may provide insight and instruction on how to repair our tattered and torn social fabric. Sketched in this eighty-seven-minute animated movie is a framework for great parenting. Examining *The Lion King* can create and change the standards and expectations of parents.

If, for some strange reason, you don't find *The Lion King* as compelling as I do, I hope you would, at the very least, acknowledge that all parents should love and instruct their children the way Mufasa loved and raised Simba.

Finally, I hope after reviewing the first ten rules, you will admit that our future rests squarely on the shoulders of parents understanding how and remaining committed to raising children who are prepared and determined to leave the planet better than it was when they arrived.

Dedication

Dear Soop,

I wrote this book because being your father is the greatest joy of my life, and I hope all parents have the same delightful experience. Thank you for challenging me to do more with my time on the planet. I can't say thanks enough for the reminder that the ability to dream and capacity to make our desires a reality only expires when we do. Now because of you, I continuously imagine a better world, and as long as I have time, I promise you that I won't ever again stop working to make the world I dream of a reality.

I love you, man!

Dad

Table of Contents

PROLOGUE   11

RULE NO. 1: A FATHER MUST SHARE EQUALLY THE TASK OF RAISING A CHILD.   17

RULE NO. 2: SHARE YOUR CHILD'S LIFE WITH YOUR VILLAGE. 25

RULE NO. 3: SHARED DNA DOESN'T CONNOTE THE SHARED BEST INTEREST OF YOUR CHILDREN.   34

RULE NO. 4: DON'T MAKE A PROMISE TO YOUR CHILD THAT YOU DON'T HAVE EVERY INTENTION OF KEEPING.   43

RULE NO. 5: SET FIRM, UNMISTAKABLY EASY-TO-UNDERSTAND PARAMETERS.   50

RULE NO. 6: TELL YOUR CHILDREN THE TRUTH ABOUT IMPORTANT THINGS LIKE LIFE AND DEATH.   59

RULE NO. 7: GIVE YOUR CHILD A NAME THAT HAS PREDICTIVE PURPOSE.   70

RULE NO. 8: YOUR CHILD IS A NARCISSIST.   82

RULE NO. 9: TRAIN YOUR CHILD TO BE A GREAT CITIZEN.   89

RULE NO. 10: FAILURE IS NOT A CHILD'S BEST WAY TO LEARN 97

REFERENCES 108

IT'S A JUNGLE OUT THERE

Prologue

Just Can't-Wait...To Be King: What I Learned From The Lion King (Originally appeared on the blog The Raising Supaman Project, November 15, 2011)

In the Beginning

On a Friday evening, June 24, 1994, I went to see a movie opening at my local theater. Unfortunately, unlike my amazing jet-setting sister, I wasn't invited to the Hollywood premiere where I could marvel at all the celebrities walking down the red carpet. I was simply buying a ticket – or so I mistakenly thought – to watch just another movie.

This movie had been hyped all winter and spring. The critics claimed that it was groundbreaking for its utilization of computers and 3-D imaging. The film went on to win a host of awards. Unbeknownst to me, at the time that I entered the theater, I was about to see something that would have a profound effect on my life.

The Lion King: When a Movie is More Than Entertainment

That evening I watched the most inspiring story that I had ever seen; a story about the love a father had for his son, a story about a father teaching his son how to be a true leader and a story where a son comes to fully understand his awesome responsibility to not only himself but

Nathaniel A. Turner, J.D., MALS

to the greater humanity. I saw a story that June evening where a son placed great value on his father's life and where the father was not only the son's hero but a best friend.

The movie captured what I know now as some of the highs and lows of parenting. The film today has encouraged me to start writing a second book on the rules of parenting (more about that later). The movie which I am referring to was recently re-released, and I highly recommend it to all fathers.

On June 24, 1994, one year and three days from the day my Benevolent King aka Supaman was born (June 27, 1995), I watched a movie which not only helped me realize how much I actually looked forward to being a father but I saw something that encapsulated the type of relationship I hoped to have with my child. The movie that changed my life was none other than Disney's animation "The Lion King."

A Man's Law Violation

By my admission that I voluntarily and willingly bought a ticket to watch a children's animated movie, I know that I have probably broken another one of those "Man Laws." Truth be told, I will almost certainly violate several other "Man Laws" throughout the life of this blog. While I am confessing to another "Man Law" indiscretion, I may as well plead guilty to the internal feelings and external expressions of laughter, sadness, anger, stillness, exhilaration, and

It's A Jungle Out There

disappointment I experienced while watching The Lion King.

I was guilty of many more counts of "Man Law" violation, as I sat motionless in the theater when the movie ended. While the credits rolled across the screen and the other viewers exited the theater, I wanted to exit as well, but I could not move. At that moment, I was only able to muster enough energy to lower my head so that I could avoid being seen. Contrary to what you might be thinking, I did not lower my head out of embarrassment.

I felt no shame in being in a theater that was almost exclusively occupied by small children and their parents. I lowered my head because I was crying uncontrollably. I had no immediate explanation for what was occurring, but I was crying like one does when they find out someone they love has passed.

Surely, the death of an animated Lion could not elicit the same emotions as the loss of a living breathing human being. What in the world was wrong with me? Suddenly it hit me like Rafiki hits Simba on the head with his stick. I had been emotionally jarred by the depiction of the kind of relationship I longed to share with my own father.

Children of All Ages Need Fathers

The movie reminded me of just how fractured my relationship was with my father. For the

Nathaniel A. Turner, J.D., MALS

initial few moments that the crowd exited the theater, I had a profound sense of hopelessness. I feared any hope of ever experiencing the type of unconditional love that I had just watched. Almost as quickly as my feelings of foreboding had appeared, I started to feel strangely optimistic. My tears went from tears of angst to tears of joy.

As I pondered my rapidly changing emotions, I realized the movie was about a father and his newborn son and not about a middle-aged father and his twenty-something son. I realized that while my father and I might never be able to share the relationship that Mufasa and Simba shared, my child and I could.

The Pledge: To Be King

At that precise moment, I pledged to God, myself, and the child that I would someday have that I would be Mufasa, and my child would be Simba. For nearly seventeen years, for each and every millisecond of every day, I have lived out that pledge like the one incontrovertible truth in my life, and I have lived my promise and will continue to do so unashamedly, unapologetically and without equivocation.

From the instant that I knew my son had been conceived to this very moment, I have loved my son as profoundly and as purposeful as Mufasa loved Simba.

It's A Jungle Out There

On that memorable day in June, I first understood on the deepest level what is expected of one who is to be called "dad" and "father." As I sat in my theater seat crying like an overgrown baby, I recognized that until the day I die, and my body becomes the grass that the antelope eat, I am responsible for making sure that my son knows and remembers:

1. who he is;
2. that he knows I am his pal;
3. that he knows he is the descendant of great kings and queens;
4. that he knows I will protect and defend him against anything and anyone;
5. that he knows that the world is his and all the opportunities that he can conceive;
6. that he knows there are consequences for every action or inaction;
7. that he understands as a true king – he must practice obedience and patience;
8. that he knows that there are limits to where and how far he should go;
9. that he knows it is a must for him to have a great appreciation for all living things and
10. that he knows that even when my physical presence has departed from this earth, I will always be with him.

In one hour and twenty-seven minutes, The Lion King crystallized all the responsibilities of a father for me. Thanks to an animated movie, I had a renewed spirit and hope for my life and the future. My tears of pain had turned into tears of joy. I realized that I was not doomed to

Nathaniel A. Turner, J.D., MALS

suffer the poor relationship with my father as I understood that just like Mufasa, I could have a son who I could raise to be king.

Rule No. 1: A Father Must Share Equally the Task of Raising a Child.

As a man who has watched a woman give birth to my offspring no less, I can say without equivocation that women are the stronger gender. Women via genetics have involuntarily inherited a job that most men could never endure – a position that would undeniably remain vacant even if men were physically capable of performing the duties as assigned.

Women single-handedly embrace the unenviable responsibility of having to be the exclusive physical host for another life for nine long, arduous months. This phenomenal solo obligation is something that should not be taken lightly by anyone, especially not a man.

Consider for a moment all the things that happen to a pregnant woman. Pregnancy not only brings with it the exhilarating expectation of another life but expecting mothers have the sole obligation of having to contend with a litany of physical and emotional issues. During pregnancy, a woman's body is changed and disturbed from the top of her head down to the bottom of her feet.

The following are but a few of the most common physical, mental, and emotional issues of pregnancy. These issues do not exist in the lives of fathers, no matter how participatory a man may be during pregnancy. In fact, most men are oblivious to these issues, and only a few men care about the pain and suffering of pregnancy. The "mandatory host of the father's children" endures excruciating discomfort and constant misery (The Liz Library 2012):

- exhaustion
- altered appetite and senses of taste and smell
- nausea and vomiting
- heartburn and indigestion
- constipation
- weight gain
- dizziness and light-headedness
- bloating, swelling, fluid retention
- hemorrhoids
- abdominal cramps
- yeast infections
- congested, bloody nose
- acne and mild skin disorders
- skin discoloration
- mild to severe backaches and strains
- increased headaches
- difficulty sleeping and discomfort while sleeping
- increased urination and incontinence
- bleeding gums
- pica
- breast pain and discharge
- swelling of joints, leg cramps, joint pain
- problems sitting, standing in later pregnancy
- inability to take regular medications

It's A Jungle Out There

- shortness of breath
- higher blood pressure
- hair loss
- tendency to anemia
- curtailment of the ability to participate in some sports and activities
- infection including those from severe and potentially fatal disease
- immune deficiency, making them more susceptible to fungal and other diseases
- extreme pain on delivery
- hormonal mood changes, including normal post-partum depression
- continued post-partum exhaustion and recovery period
- stretch marks (worse in younger women)
- loose skin
- permanent weight gain or redistribution
- abdominal and vaginal muscle weakness
- pelvic floor disorder
- changes to breasts
- varicose veins
- scarring from episiotomy or C-section
- other permanent aesthetic changes to the body
- an increased proclivity for hemorrhoids
- loss of dental and bone calcium; cavities and osteoporosis

Based on the litany of physical and emotional problems a mother can encounter because of pregnancy, the father must be prepared to assume the *compulsory accountable parent* role. The very moment a woman gives birth – not one

Nathaniel A. Turner, J.D., MALS

second longer – her days of having to be solely responsible for the physical, mental, and emotional well-being of the child must come to a baby-screaming halt.

Like Mufasa, the moment the child is born, the moment a child first breathes outside the womb, men must immediately get engaged in their new and all-important role as a father, as a *compulsory accountable parent.* Men must, like Mufasa, be by the mother's side the moment the child is born. Men must be committed – at that very moment when they learn that they are going to be fathers – to be fully involved in their child's life for as they both shall live.

While I have no scientific proof of this, I can't help but believe that a child's entry into the world is enhanced when a child opens their eyes to find the two people responsible for creating them looking happy and lovingly back at them. I do not doubt that there is an excitement associated with seeing the mother and grandmother, the mother and aunt, the mother and friend, or some other combination of parent and villager. Based exclusively on the look I remember seeing on my son's face, I find it hard to believe a happier look ever exists than the look a child has when they look at their father standing with their mother as they enter the world. Although it would be naïve to believe that all relationships that create life are going to be the result of a happily-ever-after marriage, it is imperative that men, notwithstanding, be

It's A Jungle Out There

actively connected to their children as soon as possible for as long as possible.

Fathers are much more important than many parents realize, and fathers are more important than countless parents desire to acknowledge. Men must remember that even where there is no romantic relationship or domestic commitment to the mother, we must always honor our genetic contract with our children. Without this type of covenant, neighborhoods, cities, states, and countries will continue to suffer.

According to the U.S. Census Bureau, 24 million children in America – one out of three – live in biological father-absent homes. (National Fatherhood Initiative 2012) One out of every three children in America has a father who does not understand, welcome, or celebrate his essential role. The effects of the father's absence are evident in every aspect of society:

- Children in father-absent homes are almost four times more likely to be poor. In 2011, 12 percent of children in married-couple families were living in poverty, compared to 44 percent of children in mother-only families. (National Fatherhood Initiative 2012)
- Premature infants who have increased visits from their fathers during hospitalization have improved weight gain and score higher on developmental tests. (National Fatherhood Initiative 2012)

- Babies with involved fathers experience throughout the pregnancy experience fewer complications during birth. (National Fatherhood Initiative 2012)
- Children who live apart from their fathers are more likely to be diagnosed with asthma and experience an asthma-related emergency even after factoring demographic and socioeconomic conditions. (National Fatherhood Initiative 2012)
- A 2002 Department of Justice survey of 7,000 inmates revealed that 39% of jail inmates lived in mother-only households. (National Fatherhood Initiative 2012)
- Single parenthood ratios were strongly correlated with violent crimes in a study of INTERPOL crime statistics of 39 countries. Such a correlation did not exist 18 years ago. (National Fatherhood Initiative 2012)
- Researchers using a pool from both the U.S. and New Zealand found substantial evidence that father absence escalates early sexual activity and teenage pregnancy. Early sexual activity is twice as likely to occur, and adolescent pregnancy is seven times more likely among teens whose fathers are not present. (National Fatherhood Initiative 2012)
- Girls whose parents separated between birth and six years old experienced twice the risk of early menstruation, more than four times the risk of early sexual

It's A Jungle Out There

- intercourse, and two and a half times higher risk of early pregnancy when compared to girls raised in intact families. The longer a woman lived with both parents, the lower her risk of early reproductive development. (Quinlan 2003)
- The National Longitudinal Survey of Youth found that obese children are more likely to live in father-absent homes than are non-obese children. (National Fatherhood Initiative 2012)
- A study revealed that youth who have experienced divorce, separation, or a nonunion birth have significantly higher levels of behavioral problems in school than do children who have always lived with both biological parents. (National Fatherhood Initiative 2012)

The aforementioned staggering statistics are just a sprinkling of the multitude of examples concerning the adverse societal effects which occur when fathers are absent and are not active participants in the lives of their children. Pride Land, the fictional setting of the movie, did not suffer the societal issues we experience because Mufasa, until his death, was present and accountable for Simba.

Mufasa was present the moment Sarabi gave birth to Simba. Mufasa did not once leave Simba's side. Mufasa's connection with his son was so secure that it continued even after his death.

Nathaniel A. Turner, J.D., MALS

Real-life fathers must be like Mufasa, who established a loving, nurturing, validating, and everlasting bond with Simba. Our children, our neighborhoods, our cities, our states, our country, and the world cannot afford for fathers to do anything less.

Rule No. 2: Share Your Child's Life with Your Village.

There are many challenges to being a parent. Many of the difficulties originate from the advent and proliferation of technology – computers, smartphones, the internet, satellite, etc.

Among the beneficial things about our technological devices is that they have permitted the revelation of things we might otherwise have gone a lifetime not knowing. Technology reduces, in many ways, the enormity of the world.

Thanks to technological advances, the world in all its breadth can be made small for children. More than at any other time in the history of the world, today, we can expose children to so much. Children can see parts of the world that they could previously only read about in a book. Children can communicate with people on the other side of the world just as quickly as they can with those in their own homes.

However, all this technological access, while exciting and enlightening, should not be misunderstood as confirmation that children no longer need to be parented. In truth, exposing children to so much information reveals an even greater need for the presence of parents. Parenting is required to aid children as they process and discern much of the information that they would otherwise be left to sort out on their own.

As remarkable as technology may be, the continuity and success of society still require a human touch and personal interaction. Technological advancement will never be a substitute for parenting. Regrettably, many parents routinely delegate technology as their proxy for parental instruction or competent adult supervision.

In many ways, technology outsourced parenting has become an accepted norm – normal for parents, confounding for children, and treacherous for society. So many children are now expected to care for themselves, and far too many are compelled to do so, based on technology and their own undeveloped and underdeveloped abilities. According to The American Academy of Child and Adolescent Psychiatry (AACAP):

> Every day thousands of children arrive home from school to an empty house. Every week thousands of parents make decisions to leave children home alone while they go to work, run errands, or for social engagements. It is estimated over 40% of children are left home at some time, though rarely overnight. In more extreme situations, some children spend so much time without their

It's A Jungle Out There

> parents that these children are labeled "latchkey children," referring to the house, or apartment key strung visibly around their neck... (American Academy of Child and Adolescent Psychiatry 2017)

As if leaving our children home alone with only a technological device is not scary and dangerous enough, it appears that a fracturing American family makes the lives of many of our children increasingly tricky. According to the U.S. Census Bureau, more than a quarter of our children live with only one of their parents. (United States Census Bureau 2011)

Having only one parent is not just disheartening for our children, but it increases a child's chances of living in poverty. Children who live with a single mother live at or below the poverty line 27% of the time. (Wolf 2018) Children with a single father live at or below the poverty line, 12.9% of the time. (Wolf 2018) In total, nearly four out of every ten children raised in a single-parent household lives in poverty.

I'm confident that I am not disclosing new secrets when I tell you there are consequences to living in poverty. Children who live in poverty are more likely to suffer from low academic achievement, to drop out of school, and to have health, behavioral, and emotional problems. (Child Trends Databank 2015)

As should be overwhelmingly clear from the indicators above, the outcomes associated with leaving children at home alone to be parented by technological devices and the correlation to living in poverty are much too dire to ignore. Based on the data, now is as good a time as ever to have a village that will help raise our children – a community to help develop our children so that our children are not rearing themselves.

I'm sure you have heard the age-old expression, "It takes a village to raise a child." You might think that in the 21st century, such a declaration is obsolete. On the contrary, this expression remains as valid today as at any previous time in history.

If you didn't acknowledge it before, hopefully, you do now – the world is far too complicated and too demanding to raise your child single-handedly. I don't care who you think you are, at some point, even with technology, every parent needs human help. And every parent would be well-served to be a part of a village.

It might seem like common sense, but because reason is not all that common, it must be emphatically stated: just any village members won't do. Sure, we need help from the village to raise our children, but we need

It's A Jungle Out There

the "right villagers" – villagers are not all created equal.

Our children need and deserve dependable, engaged, and skilled villagers who vow to put children first. Wisdom tells us that neither our children nor the greater society can continue to accept assistance from residents the likes of the town drunk or village idiot.

What is absolutely imperative and mandatory moving forward is that the villagers who assist in the rearing of our children be the "right villagers." Merely accepting the assistance from all who reside in the village to help raise our children has proven time and again to be a colossal mistake – a blunder of epic proportions that continues to tear at the fabric of our nation.

For children to reach their potential, they will need the aid of the "right villagers" – supportive, committed people who can and will only add value to our children's lives. From the moment our children enter the world, we should have already predetermined who the "right villagers" will be. We should have a list of those we trust and consider the most prepared to add value to our child's life.

Mufasa's actions in the opening scene illustrate the process of selecting the "right villager" and introducing them to the children. Mufasa begins forecasting who the "right villagers" are in the opening scene. In

Nathaniel A. Turner, J.D., MALS

this scene, Mufasa hands Simba to Rafiki, who prepares Simba for a formal introduction to the village. Once Simba is consecrated, Rafiki walks to the highest point of Pride Rock, where he holds Simba with outstretched arms for the entire community to see.

Those villagers who were the "right villagers" stood and cheered Simba's arrival, while the wrong villagers like Uncle Scar and the hyenas neither cheered Simba's birth nor were they present at the ceremony.

The opening scene reveals that the "right villagers" do not include jealous, depraved relatives, or heinous village residents. The "right villagers" are like those who stood at the foot of Pride Rock watching and waiting eagerly for the arrival and celebration of Simba.

Once your child is born, delicately, and cautiously like Rafiki extends Simba outstretched from the top of Pride Rock to the skillful and beneficial guidance Zazu provides Simba, you will be able to discriminate (if you haven't done so already) who your child's "right villagers" are. Your child's "right villagers" – just like Simba's "right villagers" – will stand by your side, delivering the quality of care to your children routinely reserved for royalty.

It's A Jungle Out There

Although *The Lion King* is a work of fiction, the mindset and qualities of the "right villagers" are real. "Right villagers" will gladly provide the same regal standard of care afforded to Simba and will do so for the very reason the villagers of the Pride Land did. "Right villagers" will care for your children lovingly because they believe in the Circle of Life and know that they cannot live forever. "Right villagers" are motivated by the idea that the goal of all living creatures should be to leave the world no less than it was when they inherited it, but more aptly, they should leave it a better place than they received it.

Furthermore, the "right villagers" believe all children are of equal importance. "Right villagers" readily understand that there are no limits to what a child can accomplish, nor are there any restrictions on the heights the village can reach when all children receive the proper training and support. Even when tempted to act selfishly, "right villagers" will not because they understand the direct connection that the maturation, growth, and success of all children has on the future of the village and themselves.

"Right villagers" don't have to be poked or prodded to be invested or involved in your child's life, which makes them easy to detect. "Right Villagers believe every child, regardless of race, gender, ability, class or socioeconomic standing, possess the potential to be a future leader who impacts

Nathaniel A. Turner, J.D., MALS

not only the village but their own life favorably. Your "right villagers" are people who would never want to be responsible for keeping any child from reaching their fullest potential – becoming a great leader, a transcendent visionary, or someone capable of changing the world and the course of history.

As specific as the description of a "right villager," it's noteworthy that "right villagers" are ubiquitous. Many times, they are immediate and extended family members. Sometimes they are friends and business colleagues. Occasionally they are community leaders and mentors. Whoever and wherever they are, you must identify them and utilize them as soon as humanly possible.

Good thing for Simba and Pride Land that Mufasa did not wait until tomorrow to identify the "right villagers" because tomorrow might have been too late. Mufasa understood the urgency and necessity of identifying "right villagers." He recognized that Simba's well-being and the future of Pride Land depended on the continuity and investment of the village, Simba's extended support system.

A study titled "The Social Influences on the Realization of Genetic Potential for Intellectual Development" supports what appears to be Mufasa's thoughts and actions about "right villagers." (Guang Guo 2002) In

It's A Jungle Out There

the study, the authors hypothesized that the extent to which a child realizes his or her genetic potential depends on the socio-economic environment.

In the real world, the authors theorized what Mufasa already knew to be true: children have the highest chance to realize their fullest potential when surrounded by the "right villagers."

Rule No. 3: Shared DNA Doesn't Connote the Shared Best Interest of Your Children.

In scene two, Mufasa has an intense discussion with his brother Scar about Scar's absence from Simba's Birth Ceremony. As the scene ends, Zazu, Mufasa's majordomo, attempts to console Mufasa about the tenuous relationship he has with his brother Scar. Zazu tells Mufasa, "there is one in every family, Sire, two in mine, actually, and they always manage to ruin special occasions."

Zazu's words not only foreshadow the treachery that will soon befall Simba, Mufasa, and the Pride Land, but Zazu's words give insight into something that we all know and have most likely experienced – something that while being conscious of, we are typically too embarrassed to admit.

Not everyone with our DNA wants what's best for us. Not everyone who shares our DNA wants us to experience joy or happiness. The truth found in Zazu's words is that sometimes the biggest roadblock to life's good fortune is not located on life's highway. Instead, there are times when the main barricade to our best experience is an unwelcome family member standing in our driveway.

If, as a society, we are willing to drop the façade of pretending that we all have perfect families,

It's A Jungle Out There

we might accomplish what Mufasa was unable to do – prevent irreversible harm from coming to us, those we love and the larger society. If we could be real with ourselves, most of us would admit that we have at least one relative, that is, to put it mildly, "not all there."

Each of us probably knows someone who shares our DNA, who might even look just like us, who is only happy when we are unhappy – a blood relative that seems hell-bent on making life calamitous for all that cross their path. In politically correct terms, I'm talking about a family member who is at a minimum "one fry short of a Happy Meal."

Because I genuinely believe that "acceptance is the first step to recovery," I will start with an admission of my own. There is at least one member of my family that is "crazy as a Betsy bug." When I say crazy, I mean insane as H-E-double-hockey-sticks. I'm talking about the proverbial village idiot. This family member's behavior is so inexplicably offensive that if you googled the words "outrageously bizarre," his image would appear.

For years, during every family gathering, holiday, birthday, reunion, and any other family event, I subjected myself, just like the rest of my family, to the rude manners of my "crazy as H-E-double-hockey-sticks" relative. Everyone endured his abusive and disturbing behavior because no one wanted to "make waves" or, worse, be the family exile.

Nathaniel A. Turner, J.D., MALS

My family's theoretical approach was to "ignore" him whenever he had an outburst. We all ignored his behavior as if acknowledging that he was nuts would somehow place us in the same Planter's bag with him.

However, ignoring him became progressively more challenging – profanity and threats of violence comprised his outbursts. The more I sat quietly listening to his rants and threats, the more perturbed I became. Sensing that no one in the family would ever take a stand, his belligerence and verbal assaults grew progressively worse with time.

It would be an understatement if I said I believed he needed professional help. I knew he needed professional aid, and so did all the other sane family members. But no one did anything, we all acted as if we confronted him we were going to be exiled from the family. Banished right into a straitjacket and a rubber room should have been his fate, exiled from the family long ago.

Just like Mufasa, I was repeatedly holding my tongue and saying nothing, worrying about my expulsion from future family gatherings. But then on Thanksgiving Day 1997, my patience or maybe more accurately my stupidity in enduring his nonsense and aggression came to an end. There, my immediate and extended family sat around the table. My son, having gone to the bathroom, walked back into the kitchen. As he returned to his chair, my "one fry short of a

It's A Jungle Out There

Happy Meal" relative had one of his all-too-familiar outbursts.

The rant started with allegations that my then two-year-old son had intentionally stepped on his foot and that I had somehow set in motion this devious plot – a plot to have a toddler who wore a size one shoe injure him somehow by stepping on his Sasquatch-sized foot. His rant turned to a more menacing and sadistic diatribe when he threatened to "beat my son's ass."

Initially, the entire family sat, shocked and silent. I'm sure no one could believe that a grown man 50 years my son's senior, weighing 200-plus pounds more and who stood five feet taller, had just threatened to beat a toddler. I was stunned.

Had he just threatened to beat my only begotten son? Did he think that I would ever allow him to touch my child? Was he so out of his mind that he could not acknowledge an unintentional error made by a toddler? Did he not hear my son willingly recognize his mistake and immediately apologize?

As those questions went through my mind, I waited to collect my thoughts rather than acting on my initial instincts and emotions. I could not be the father that I hoped to be for my son from behind prison bars. All the same, that eruption was the last straw for me.

Nathaniel A. Turner, J.D., MALS

I collected my immediate family and made a promise to avoid being in my "crazy as a Betsy bug" relative's company as much as I could. DNA or not, I would not do as my extended family had done and continued to do. I would not do as Mufasa had mistakenly and fatally done. Unlike the way Mufasa handled his relationship with Scar, the relationship with my own Uncle Scar was over.

While I didn't possess the legal power or kingly authority for exile or to sentence him to an institution where he would wear a straitjacket and live in a rubber room, I figuratively exiled him from my life. He was dead to me, and I would never again make excuses or concessions for his irrational and offensive behavior.

As I look back on that Thanksgiving Day, I am so grateful that I was able to keep my nerve and not act on my first emotions. More fortuitously, I'm glad that I was present and prepared to immediately eject my crazy relative from my life.

As data about child abuse illustrates, had I not removed my son from this situation, my crazy Uncle Scar might have scarred my son physically and emotionally. Had I mistakenly chosen Mufasa's path of suffering fools, my son might have suffered a fate like that of Simba – a fate endured by the nearly one million abused and neglected children who suffer annually at the hands of those sharing their DNA. (American Humane 2018)

It's A Jungle Out There

According to the Administration on Children, Youth and Families' *Child Maltreatment 2011Report* (U.S. Department of Health & Human Services 2012):

- 51 states reported 676,569 victims of child abuse and neglect; 9.1 victims per 1,000 children in the population
- Victims in the age group of birth to one year had the highest rate of victimization at 21.2 per 1,000 children
- 51 states reported a total of 1,545 fatalities
- The overall rate of child fatalities was 2.1 deaths per 100,000 children
- Four-fifths (81.6%) of all child fatalities were younger than four years old
- One or more parents caused Four-fifths (78.3%) of child fatalities

The data provided by the *Child Maltreatment 2011 Report* only tells part of the story. At first glance, the data might appear to be only sterile, extraneous figures. On closer examination combining the Child Maltreatment Report with the facts provided by Child Help, a non-profit organization dedicated to helping those affected most by child abuse and neglect, we learn of a shameful plague secretly afflicting America and her children. Child Help gives the following account: (Children's Bureau 2012)

- Every ten seconds, there is a report of child abuse.

Nathaniel A. Turner, J.D., MALS

- More than five children die every day because of child abuse.
- More than 90% of juvenile sexual abuse victims know their perpetrator in some way.
- Child abuse occurs at every socioeconomic level, across ethnic and cultural lines, within all religions and at all levels of education.
- About 30% of abused and neglected children will later abuse their children, continuing the horrible cycle of abuse.
- About 80% of 21-year-olds who abused as children met criteria for at least one psychological disorder.
- The estimated annual cost of child abuse and neglect in the United States for 2008 was $124 billion.
- Men abused as children make up 14% of all men in U.S. prisons.
- Women abused as children make up 36% of all women in U.S. prisons.
- Child abuse and neglect survivors are 59% more likely to be arrested as a juvenile, 28% more likely to be arrested as an adult, and 30% more likely to commit a violent crime.
- Abused children are 25% more likely to experience teen pregnancy.
- Abused teens are less likely to practice safe sex, putting them at higher risk for STDs.

On that Thanksgiving Day, without knowing the disgraceful facts and figures that I now know, I

It's A Jungle Out There

understood why the United States has the worst record in the industrialized world for the care and protection of children. (Children's Bureau 2012) Like Mufasa's mishandling of his relationship with Scar, we spend too much energy being concerned about the unstable adults who share our genetic material and not about the fact a child sharing our DNA has the potential of being a victim of child abuse every ten seconds. (Children's Bureau 2012) More than five children die every day as a result of child abuse while we contemplate how it might look if we publicly admit that someone in our family is unhinged. (Children's Bureau 2012) To put it plain and simple, we don't pay adequate attention to children.

Since that fateful day, I have promised not to make the same mistake that Mufasa made – ignoring and minimizing the potential of my flesh and blood to do evil. I hope Mufasa's death, the information about child abuse and the related facts, validate for you what they confirmed for me.

Our children and nation, like Simba and Pride Land, cannot afford for parents to go on pretending that our dysfunctional families are perfect, nor can we afford to have parents devote time and energy contemplating public image when exiling disturbed, dangerous family members is necessary. Like Pride Land acknowledged when Simba returned, the community not only recovers but functions so much better when we first recognize the

Nathaniel A. Turner, J.D., MALS

wayward relatives for who they really are and then exile them from our children's lives.

Rule No. 4: Don't Make a Promise to Your Child that You Don't Have Every Intention of Keeping.

In the Sunrise/Pouncing Scene, there is an interaction in which every parent has familiarity. The scene begins with a child barging into their parent's bedroom early in the morning. Well, Simba doesn't rush into a bedroom, he charges into his parent's cave, but you get the analogy.

At any rate, focused solely on one thing, Simba jumps over and even lands on a few of the lionesses sleeping in the cave. With absolutely no regard for anything or anyone else, running and jumping towards his dad like someone trying to win an obstacle course race, Simba exclaims persistently, "Dad! Da-ad! Come on, Dad, we gotta go. Dad? Da-ad. Dad, Dad, Dad, Dad, Dad, Dad, Dad, Dad--Wake up! Dad? Da-ad! Come on, Dad!" Mufasa, groggy but beginning to wake, hears his son calling his name. That's when Simba yells out those words all children can't wait to say to their parents. "You promised!"

Mufasa made Simba a promise earlier, and Simba had arrived at his father's cave at the agreed-upon time, expecting his father to be awake and ready to fulfill his promise. Based on Mufasa still being asleep and his statement to Sarabi that "before sunrise, he's YOUR son," I guess had Simba not come charging into the cave Mufasa would still have been sleeping.

Nathaniel A. Turner, J.D., MALS

However, Simba, like most children, was having none of that. Mufasa had made his son a promise and come heck or high water, Simba expected that promise to be fulfilled. Mufasa had uttered two simple words that woke a young lion before the crack of dawn; two simple words that mean everything to a child: "YOU PROMISED."

If the significance of the words "you promised" is not yet clear, I will restate it for you: children, your children especially, expect you to honor your promises NO MATTER WHAT.

Mufasa learned at the crack of dawn that if he made a promise to his son, he had better mean it. Most parents may already know that children expect us to keep our promises. However, it is unclear how many parents truly appreciate the significance of their commitments.

It doesn't matter how big or small the promise. If you promise to do something, you had better be prepared to follow through. If you promise to do something virtuous like buy your child a new video game or even if you promise to punish them for some misdeed if you say you are going to do something, make sure that you do what you said.

Now don't get me wrong, I know there are times when there are no options other than breaking a promise. Sometimes "life happens." Try as we

It's A Jungle Out There

might there are times when there is just no way around breaking a promise.

For this reason, I did not suggest that a parent's mandate should be "don't ever make a promise that you can't keep." Children can be reasonable; thus, when inopportune promissory anomalies occur, your child will surprise you.

They won't lose their cool or act in some uncivilized manner. Instead, children will show fantastic resolve by being reasonably amicable. Children will let you off the hook for your failure to keep your commitment as long as breaking your promises is rare.

Remember, you have a one-time mulligan. Just like in golf, you get one time to replay an errant shot and pretend that you didn't make an error. Nothing gets recorded on your score sheet; it's as if everyone was blindfolded and didn't see your blunder. Your children will provide you with this same courtesy, although you might only receive it once every eighteen years rather than every eighteen holes.

Your child will grant you a mulligan on your only broken promise, not like casual golf does for any old errant shot. Your child will only excuse the broken promise in the most exceptional situations.

For example, if the car breaks down 1,000 miles from home, your return flight from your overseas trip is delayed or maybe if you suffered a medical emergency that required you to be hospitalized. In such cases, your child will graciously forgive you and show you the type of leniency only reserved for a trusted confidant.

Be careful, though! Don't press your luck and have routine car trouble, which includes a car breaking down 999 miles or less from home. Don't even think of asking for forgiveness if your overseas flight is less than 5,000 miles. The same goes for medical issues. You are required to have major surgery. Your child could care less about insignificant injuries like broken bones.

Remember, breaking a promise once is a mulligan, breaking a promise twice is an excuse, and breaking a promise three times is a habit. If breaking promises becomes habitual, your child will be giving you some parental advice. Before long, you might get the lectures you have given them on the subject of proper preparation or the one about the parent who cried wolf.

Don't be surprised if you find your child not only telling you that you need to get a new car that won't break down, but you might find them searching online for your replacement car. Delayed flights will be unforgivable, and you might be informed that in the future, you should factor in flight delays and airline on-time rankings when you plan your trips. In regards to your emergency health matter, you will discover that your child is your new, competent nutritionist and personal trainer.

It's A Jungle Out There

There will be no toleration of your typical excuses. Outside of those examples above and a few similar situations, breaking your promise to your child might be the worst thing you can do. Breaking your commitments to your child establishes you as a person your child considers unreliable.

Reliability is key. I can't stress enough how significant dependability is to children. Remarkably, dependability seems not to matter when your children can't remember to do the things that they promised to do. Ask them if they cleaned their room, folded the clothes, or washed the dishes, and you likely will hear the words, "I forgot." Don't do what you said you would; you will feel the fury of those two words, "you promised."

I suppose this double standard is just another element in the Great Circle of Life. The mini versions of us have excellent memories when it is something they want, but they don't always possess the sharpest minds when it is something they promised to deliver. And just like the full-sized versions of themselves on which they pattern their lives, adults are also incredibly affected when promises made to us are broken.

No matter how much we try as adults to hide our true feelings, there is no denying we experience hurt when promises made to us are broken. Even the most mature, cynical, and thick-skinned among us are disappointed when the promises made to us are broken.

Don't believe me? Think about how you view politics and politicians. Most of us have little faith in politicians, yet we continue to hold out hope every time that we go to the polls that those who have consistently disappointed us in the past will finally keep their promises.

A poll conducted by the Pew Research Center validates this point. The Pew Research Center, an American think tank that provides information on topics, thoughts, and developments affecting the United States and the world, found that Americans' distrust of the Government is at 80%. Eight out of every ten Americans state that they have some reservations about believing anything that the Government says it will do. (Thompson 2010) Eight out of ten Americans have given politicians at least one mulligan, only to find the politicians requesting another mulligan time and again.

Despite this stated distrust of 80%, nearly 60% of eligible voters participated in the 2008 Presidential Election. (Answers.com 2012) That is six out of every ten qualified voters who, despite their overwhelming distrust of the Government, still found voting to be a worthwhile exercise. In other words, even the most skeptical and disillusioned among us are just like children. We always want to believe in other people's ability to make and keep promises.

It's A Jungle Out There

The small versions of us are carbon copies, or more accurately DNA replicas. They hold out hope as long as possible, expecting and praying that promises will be kept. As parents, we have to do a better job of keeping our promises.

We promise our children that no child will be left behind. Broken promise. We guarantee our children that they will be healthy. Broken promise. We promise our children that they can go to and from school safely. Broken promise. We promise our children that we will be home early from work. Broken promise. We pledge to our children that we will go outside and play with them instead of falling asleep on the couch. Broken promise.

Maybe we should again take our direction from Mufasa. Even in death, Mufasa remained with Simba as he had promised. Mufasa made his word his bond.

Great parents don't function like the Government. Great parents don't request multiple mulligans. Great parents do not make a habit of promising anything that they have concerns about delivering. Great parents like Mufasa let their word be their bond – they make sure that their word lives forever.

Rule No. 5: Set Firm, Unmistakably Easy-to-Understand Parameters.

Spend a few minutes in the presence of a small child, and it won't take long to understand what the word *inquisitive* means. Inquisitive – always asking a thousand questions and not being able to accept an answer to any question without following it up with "why?" or "my friend gets to do it."

If you have a teenager, you might also recognize this dialogue. Although teenagers don't talk to you as much as small children. But I digress.

Forgive me; I got a little ahead of myself. I'm presently experiencing the probing existence of a teenager. It's rough! If you haven't already experienced it, all I can say is that your day is coming. If you have experienced it, we should form a support group and commiserate together.

At any rate, let me return my attention to the good old preschool days. As I think back to the time when my son was an infant, I can remember watching his eyes light up and him breaking his neck, trying desperately to get a glimpse of the source of every sound that he heard.

As a toddler, not only was he still breaking his neck to associate the sound with sight, but he was also beginning to ask questions about what he heard and saw. Rarely was a simple answer

It's A Jungle Out There

sufficient or satisfactory. A response to his questions almost always required the type of explanation professors demand when their students are defending a doctoral thesis.

Even trying to talk to him about his safety was a supervisory nightmare. Instruction about daily dangers like not running down the stairs, keeping his hands away from a hot stove, not playing in the street, or not going near electrical sockets were all met with deep suspicion and speculation. At all times, he reacted as if there was something more he should know that I wasn't telling him.

Whenever I gave him the "please be safe" directive, he would look at me curiously as if I was a great mystic who possessed the answers to the Universe and was denying him a share of my sovereign knowledge. Unbeknownst to him, I was a new father, and I knew very little about being a parent.

I was far from being the great mystic he suspected me to be. I was winging it. All I wanted in my role as a new father was to for him to be safe. No matter what I said, though, he could not accept a simple answer to any question.

One evening, we had one of those inquisitive or, in more precise terms, an exhausting conversation. Earlier in the day, I had warned him about running down the stairs. Already exhausted from the prior discussion and

Nathaniel A. Turner, J.D., MALS

beginning to feel a little frustrated, I subjected myself to the following conversation:

> Me: Son, don't run down the stairs. (Clearly frustrated)
>
> Son: Why not?
>
> Me: Because I said so! (Growing increasingly frustrated)
>
> Son: Daddy, 'because' is a conjunction – something comes before and after because.
>
> Me: I know what a conjunction is, thank you very much! Don't run down the stairs because it is dangerous and you might get hurt.
>
> Son: Daddy, how is it dangerous? How do you know I might get hurt?
>
> Me: Son, it is dangerous because you could fall and injure yourself.
>
> Son: Daddy, I won't get hurt. I run fast. I'm careful. If I do fall, I'll get a Band-Aid.
>
> Me: Son, would you please do as I asked you to do! (At my wits' end and ready to proceed with Old School Parenting – you know "go get your belt boy!")
>
> Son: Daddy, it's not fair. You must not trust me. You won't let me have any fun. (Pouting and dejected)
>
> Me: (Exhausted and silent)

Such was my life with a toddler. Thanks to my son, I learned very early in his life that children don't seem to comprehend simple answers.

It's A Jungle Out There

Moreover, learning about children's inquisitive nature was enhanced by living with a miniature professor. My pint-sized professor taught me that children prefer to 'color outside the lines.' I discovered that children only color between the lines because we tell them that they should.

As an aside, I would like to add that in some ways, I believe we stifle our children's growth by asking them to always color between the lines and not encouraging them to question everything. This is, in part, why I didn't employ the "Old School Method of Parenting" and tolerated some of these lengthy, exhausting discussions with my son.

I could have just done what my father would have done; he would have said "yes" or "no" with no other discussion outside of him, replying "go get your belt." But I didn't want to stifle my son's intellectual growth or independence. My fear – a fear greater than wanting to pass out from an extended dialogue – was that my son might end up like so many of our children who have had their inquisitive nature subdued during childhood.

Too many of our children cannot reason, and when they are supposed to be able to make the right decisions, they can't. Later in life, the same parents who muted their toddler's analytical and creative ability find themselves dissatisfied by the choices their adolescent and teenage children make and the people their children have become.

Nathaniel A. Turner, J.D., MALS

My son was no exception to wanting to color outside the line. Most children like my son want to do what they want to do when they want to do it. The key is to help them develop a capacity to learn from the questions that they ask and to establish a lifelong process for making the right decisions. Sometimes, as evidenced by Simba's unauthorized jaunt to the Elephant Graveyard, children do what they want to do regardless of what anyone else has advised, even when that advice comes from their old man.

My discussion with my son running down the stairs was similar to Mufasa's Elephant Graveyard discussion with Simba. Simba wanted to go to the Elephant Graveyard because it was fun. My son wanted to run up and down the stairs, because it was fun.

Instead of participating in a grand inquisition, I just wanted my son to "get it." I wanted him to recognize that I had lived on this earth thirty more years than he and that I understood that there were going to be times when people and societal messages encouraged him to do things that he should not do. I wanted him to know that there were always going to be temptations to do those things that are impermissible.

He was only a child, and he was not at a stage in his development where he could "get it." As such, I realized that if I was going to do an adequate job keeping him safe, I was going to

It's A Jungle Out There

have to set clear, understandable, unambiguous, age-appropriate parameters.

In this regard, my son was no different from Simba, who did not understand that there were people, places, and things that were dangerous. If Mufasa had to educate Simba about where his kingdom began and ended, I would have to make sure that my son knew that he had boundaries. And like Simba, instructing my son that he had limits by only responding to his inquisitions with answers like "yes" or "no" and "do" or "don't" was a recipe for disaster.

My mini professor unintentionally reinforced what I had learned as a child from my parents. Parents have an obligation of establishing and maintaining expectations, setting boundaries that are visible, and crystal clear.

As *The Lion King* illustrates, when those expectations are not established and maintained unambiguously, the outcome could be perilous for both the parent and child. Unfortunately for both parents and children alike, the perils children face are not limited to those in an animated film.

According to The Association for Behavioral and Cognitive Therapies (ABCT):
> The greatest risk to children's health is not cancer, heart disease, or any other form of illness. The leading killer of children in the United States is an injury. In a single year, 10,000 children under

Nathaniel A. Turner, J.D., MALS

age 15 die, 30,000 are permanently disabled, and 16 million require emergency medical care because of injuries. Children under age 4 are at special risk. (Association for Behavioral and Cognitive Therapies n.d.)

The ABCT report goes on to state that parents can predict and prevent a significant number of childhood injuries. In short, parents must, as I stated earlier, put measures in place to foresee and avoid harm. We must do this because, at the end of the day, parents are directly responsible for the well-being of their children, especially small children.

In fulfilling the obligation to protect children, parents must not only outline the expectations they have for their children, but they must also have a process in place to make sure those expectations are met and maintained. This responsibility of establishing and maintaining expectations is a bit like owning a dog and needing to install an invisible electric fence in your yard.

Before I expound on my analogy, let me take a moment to clarify that I am in no way comparing a child to a dog, nor am I advocating that you use shock treatment to electrify your child into obedience.

The point is that when you install an invisible electric fence for your dog, you do so for many of the same reasons that you explain in great detail

It's A Jungle Out There

potential dangers and consequences to your children. You want to set clear, unambiguous boundaries for your children. You want to keep your child happy and safe. You want to make life easier for you and for the others who love and care for your child.

Without these boundaries, your child will behave like the dog without the training and structure the invisible electric fence intends to provide. If those boundaries are not established and maintained, your child will likely leave the safety of your home without your permission or, worse, they may expose themselves to hazardous, life-threatening situations.

It also should go without saying that, like the untrained dog, people will not look forward to seeing your child. When your child goes anywhere outside the home, others will feel about your child as they tend to do when someone brings an untrained dog out in public; people don't want to be around a misbehaving pet or a disobedient child.

Mufasa informed Simba that he was not to go to the Elephant Graveyard, but he did not sufficiently explain why to his son. I believe the lack of explanation left an already inquisitive child ever more curious. Consequently, not only did Simba go where he was told not to go, but he persuaded Nala to accompany him. The result was that Simba and Nala were both nearly killed.

Nathaniel A. Turner, J.D., MALS

I believe this portion of the story exists to remind parents that having an inquisitive child is always going to have its positives and negatives. The positives are that your child will ask lots of questions, which means they are likely to expedite their learning process and expand their knowledge. The negatives are that your child will ask a lot of questions, which means that if the answers they get from you are insufficient and boundaries are not well-defined, they are likely to seek the complete responses on their own or from sources that will put them in harm's way.

Protect your children and give them complete and full explanations. Treat them like a stranger who is counting on you to provide them with detail directions for their expedition. The reality is that your children are strangers to this journey called life, and their travels are much improved when those of us who know the roads provide them with trustworthy, unmistakably, easy to understand directions.

Rule No. 6: Tell Your Children the Truth about Important Things like Life and Death.

Do yourself and your children a favor. Don't describe subjects like life – how it begins and ends – as if it were some fictional fantasy right out of – of all things – an animated film. Instead, explain life from conception to expiration using age-appropriate, real-life, no-nonsense terminology.

You don't have to listen to me, but you should pay attention to Mufasa. Mufasa understood the importance of a reality-based explanation of life and death. Mufasa's conversation with Simba suggests that he was a father who chose to tell his son the truth about life and death rather than falsehoods. It seems Mufasa realized the danger of not having a child prepared for something inevitable. No matter how we protest and want to pretend it not to be foreseeable, death is unavoidable. Dying is guaranteed to happen.

Mufasa's conversation with his son exhibited not only definitiveness about death but also comfort about a subject matter with which parents must themselves find emotional comfort. Before parents can be real about death with their children, they need to get real about death with themselves. Without this reality check, parents shouldn't even consider having this conversation with their children.

Nathaniel A. Turner, J.D., MALS

One could surmise that based on the ease with which Mufasa discussed death with Simba, he had already completed his reality check and established his emotional comfort. Not only was Mufasa comfortable, but he respected and valued Simba enough not to lie to him, instead preferring to tell his son the truth – the truth being that we all have an expiration date.

As dreadful as it might seem to admit this to your child, children need to know and understand that while we might not know the day nor the hour, the day will come when we shall all cease to exist. Mufasa's expression for the beginning and ending of life was called "the Great Circle of Life."

Regrettably, far too few parents are neither at ease nor as intuitive as Mufasa. Mufasa delivered an explanation about life and death that was both authentic and suitable for a child - an elucidation foreign to many parents who continue to tell their children make-believe stories about how life begins and ends; make-believe stories that parents like to call "little white (harmless) lies."

Rather than tell the truth about "the Great Circle of Life," as Mufasa did with Simba, we use all kinds of absurd euphemisms – euphemisms which, for the record, are ordinarily utilized only when discussing topics that are harsh, blunt or offensive. But what's harsh, blunt, or offensive about life and death – "the Great Circle of Life"?

It's A Jungle Out There

Instead of explaining pregnancy and birth truthfully, we tell our children that a pregnant woman "*has a bun in the oven,*" "*is in the family way,*" "*is with child,*" or maybe even that "*she was knocked up.*" The explanation about death is equally dishonest as we disclose to our children that when someone dies they have "*fallen asleep*", "*crossed over to the other side*", "*gone onto an eternal resting place*", "*gone to a better place*", "*been called to a higher service*", or perhaps we tell them that the person has "*kicked the bucket*".

We fabricate these tall tales that, in some ways, are the small and initial agents that deprive us of actualizing life – living life in the moment. These fantasies do more harm than good. They do nothing more than mislead and postpone humanity's realization that life is to be lived with attention, passion, and urgency. These illusions are especially harmful given the irrefutable reality that tomorrow is not promised to any of us.

Intuitively, we all know that tomorrow is not promised, but these euphemisms leave us apparently unable to instinctively live life in the only moment that is available – the present. Our subconscious thoughts manifest themselves in our behavior.

If there is an "other side," why worry about doing my best now when I can do my best at the "better place"? If I can get called to "higher

Nathaniel A. Turner, J.D., MALS

service," why concern myself with my conduct, expending great effort and energy today when I can save my best for when I "cross over to the eternal resting place"? I believe these euphemisms work against the best intentions of adults. If my hypothesis is correct, a more significant question that should be asked is what effect our "little white lies" have on children.

Why are we using euphemisms when there is nothing harsh, blunt, or offensive present? How do these fantastic stories serve us, our children, or the greater society? Are pretend stories about the origin and cessation of life the best way to teach children? Do we really want our children to grow up thinking of life as something to be taken seriously only when we "crossover," "get to the other side," or "get called to higher service"? Is our intention to leave our children void of the skills necessary to handle the one thing we are unequivocally sure that they will witness, experience, and endure? Do we, parents, even recognize how disingenuous and detrimental this behavior is for our children?

I know that I just asked a lot of questions, but these are only a few of the queries we must answer. We need to answer these questions so that we can make sure our children appreciate life and live each and every day to their full potential. We must also answer these questions because of the influence our "little white lies" have on our children.

It's A Jungle Out There

Dr. Victoria Talwar of the Talwar Research team and an Associate Professor at McGill University has conducted research on the reasons that children lie. Using an adage with which most of us are familiar, children lie because *"an apple doesn't fall far from the tree,"* or, in Ph.D. terminology, Dr. Talwar reports that children learn to tell untruths because we first show them how to do it. (NPR: All Things Considered 2009) According to Dr. Talwar, "we don't explicitly tell them to lie, but they see us do it. They see us tell the telemarketer, 'I'm just a guest here.' They see us boast and lie to smooth social relationships." (Bronson 2008)

Yes, you read that correctly! We, the same parents who will long for our children to be honest with us and who have an unmitigated expectation that our children will tell the truth at all times, are the ones who teach our children how to lie. Where being open and honest is the simplest way to go, we choose instead to tell our children the tallest of contrived tales.

Not only do we tell these "little white lies" when there is nothing harsh, blunt, or offensive about the truth, but we dare to look genuinely surprised, shocked, and hurt when our child concocts some unbelievable story to try to explain their misdeed or misbehavior. Dr. Talwar's research raises another question. If we don't want make-believe justifications from our children, why then do we give fantasy explanations to our children?

Nathaniel A. Turner, J.D., MALS

The answer is simple: we promulgate our "little white lie" not because life and death are harsh, blunt, or offensive topics. We transmit these "little white lies" because we don't want to have to discuss an essential real-life matter with our children. Truth be told, we are uncomfortable discussing this subject matter because our parents were uncomfortable discussing it with us. Remember, *"the apple doesn't fall far from the tree,"* so instead of having a reality-based, age-appropriate conversation, we tell our children the same euphemisms – "little white lies" – that our parents communicated to us.

It is so hard to believe that people who were knowingly given a useless, idiotic mythical explanation as children would propagate the same pointless, silly fictitious story to their own children. What's more difficult to believe is that people who are as sophisticated and technologically advanced as modern-day parents would rely on an archaic tradition to explain death and dying.

It appears that our exploitation of truth seems to have no bounds as we are equally challenged in realistically discussing the origin of life. I suppose having some anxiety over chatting about death with a child is somewhat understandable, given the lingering effect of our childhood exposure to death and dying fairytales. However, being unable to address birth and the beginning of life in a genuine, factually age-appropriate manner is far less comprehensible. Actually, not being able to

It's A Jungle Out There

discuss any of life's stages authentically is downright comical. However, our attempts to discuss death may not be quite as amusing as some of the stories we contrive to explain the beginning of life, but no matter if we are talking about "in the beginning" or "at the end," our talking points are laughable all the same.

Think about the lengths to which we go *not* to tell the truth to our children. We have invented a story about "the Stork" in place of discussing biology, not just any bird, but "the Stork." Talk about a societal struggle between evolution and creation! However, in this situation, creation implies creative writing and creative storytelling. We would rather have our children believe that a big white bird measuring 3 ½ to 4 feet in length with a wingspan of 5 to 6 feet and weighing between 5 and 10 pounds is responsible for the delivery of the most intelligent being on the planet.

This ridiculous stork baby delivery fiction is further exacerbated by asking children to make an intellectual leap to believe that this "special bird" – an animal that cannot speak, that has no hands and weighs in some cases the same as the newborn child – can find the appropriate baby for a family from somewhere in the atmosphere. But the lunacy does not end there. No, the insanity is actually just getting started.

We then want children to believe that "the Big Bird" provides food, shelter, and clothing for the baby until "the Big Bird" can find the time in its busy schedule of baby location, infant nurturing and child delivery to deliver the right baby to the correct expecting parents. Oh, and did I mention, we compel our children to believe that "the Stork" delivers the baby by dropping in on the expecting parents undetected through our chimney without injuring itself or the baby. This acrobatic daredevil feat of 'cutting-edge' baby delivery technique is performed even in homes where there is no chimney or where there is a fireplace with a roaring fire.

Last, but certainly not least, as if this whopper of a tale was not outlandish enough, we dispense with reality, once more, in the name of weight loss. Somehow, miraculously, we leave our children thinking that the moment the baby is dropped through the chimney, Mommy's stomach shrinks back to the way it looked nine months prior. Pain-free and stress-free labor with an immediate return to a pre-pregnancy body – what an unbelievably novel concept. It's too bad for the child-bearers all over the world that this concept is as believable as the story of "the Stork."

Telling and propagating these ridiculous make-believe stories only work to our disadvantage. Not only do daughters who later become mothers feel deceived when they learn that their bodies don't just snap back to pre-pregnancy string bikini levels, but your children might not find you to be credible in some other areas.

It's A Jungle Out There

In the not-too-distant future, that stork-delivered baby of yours might find it difficult to talk to you, the "resident little white liar," about things going on in their life. Your prior inability to speak honestly with them about something so simple may lead them to believe that you might be unprepared to have conversations about more challenging matters in age-appropriate, real-world terms.

Think about it: the first serious conversation that they attempted to have with you resulted in you telling them the most outrageous of tales. How comfortable would you be talking to someone about a serious subject when that same person is the person who chose *not* to speak to you honestly about something as routine and ordinary as how life is created? How likely would you be to share your fears and concerns with the person who told you that on the day you were born, "the Stork" flew on top of the roof of the house, jumped down the chimney, and handed you over to your new parents? It's one thing for your child to think you are a fool; it's another thing for you to confirm it by telling them one of these ridiculous make-believe stories.

No matter how you protest, your child is going to learn the truth about how life begins and ends from somewhere and from someone. You just might want the person who provides that explanation to be you. An insect, a pet, a sibling, a cousin, a classmate's sibling... something or

Nathaniel A. Turner, J.D., MALS

someone is going to be born and/or die, and your child will seek a real answer.

If your child is not armed in advance with the truth, eagerly waiting to provide them with an explanation will be one of their peers, a website, a video, or some other media outlet. Tell your child the truth so that they won't be alarmed and feel duped when they learn you lied to them. Don't subject your child to being the naïve child; the youngster other children tease because you failed to share the truth about something mild, gentle, and natural – life and death. Nobody – not even a small child – wants to be thought of as a fool.

So if you still can't find your own voice to explain to your child how this thing called life works, feel free to follow Mufasa's lead.

> Mufasa: A king's time as ruler rises and falls like the sun. One day, Simba, the sun will set on my time here and will rise with you as the new king.
>
> Everything you see exists together in a delicate balance. As king, you need to understand that balance and respect all the creatures, from the crawling ant to the leaping antelope.
>
> Simba: But Dad, don't we eat the antelope?

It's A Jungle Out There

> Mufasa: Yes, Simba, but let me explain. When we die, our bodies become the grass, and the antelope eat the grass. And so we are all connected in the great Circle of Life.

While I realize that Mufasa is a fictional character, his explanations are a whole lot less contrived and more realistic than most of ours. Ordinarily the summary of our account of life and death goes something like this: a mother gets a "bun in the oven" – a bun that will someday disappear right around the time that "the Stork" appears to deliver a baby, and then at some point when we are old we will "fall asleep" – "crossing over to the other side" – so that we might begin answering "our call to a higher service". You must admit this is utterly ridiculous!

Enough "white lies" already! It's time for parents to grow up and be models of the behavior we expect of our children. Today is a great day to introduce your children to something called "the truth."

Rule No. 7: Give Your Child a Name That Has Predictive Purpose.

What's in a name... everything, actually! Words are so compelling. So powerful, in fact, that English author and playwright, Edward Bulwer Lytton, coined the phrase "*the pen is mightier than the sword*." Mr. Bulwer Lytton used this expression in his play, Richelieu, to illustrate just how powerful words can be.

If you will, picture a pen, a small device of only a few inches in length and filled with ink, having power exceeding that of a sword, a sharp, dangerous weapon capable of maiming or taking life. Upon the first reflection, a pen having more power than a sword seems absurd. On the surface, anyone concerned with having to defend themselves would want to have a sword instead of a pen. However, if you look beyond the obvious, you will agree with the playwright that "*the pen is mightier than the sword.*"

A sword can threaten, defeat, and potentially kill a single opponent, but it can only do so one opponent at a time. Words, however, can change the mind of an opponent without exerting much physical energy or absent spilling any blood. Words can defeat a large army where one might have previously thought an army of swordsmen was the only option. Words make up the letter requesting aid from family, friends, or military allies who will stand by your side to show a united front when a sword is raised by your

It's A Jungle Out There

enemy. Words like those found in the Declaration of Independence, the Emancipation Proclamation, the Bill of Rights, and the Nineteenth Amendment changed the course of history for millions of people. Such is the power of words.

Words in a song reflect our feelings of love, devotion, pain, and disappointment. Words in government documents convey the promises and hopes for just and righteous leadership. Words in contracts guarantee fair and equitable treatment for all parties. At times, one word can have the same powerful effect that multiple words carry. A single word can, in fact, be more powerful than a sword.

I trust you believe as I do that, the playwright's assertion is accurate. Words have more power than a sword. Therefore, would it not be prudent to exercise equal or more exceptional care with the use of words as one would exert in wielding a sword? And although I have never brandished a sword, I know it is dangerous and would pose some hazards to me and anyone in my presence. Like we would do when holding a sword, parents need to recognize the power of words and their potential to pose significant dangers and create hazardous situations for their children.

Unfortunately, it doesn't appear that enough parents have been introduced to Edward Bulwer Lytton's play *Richelieu*. Not nearly enough, parents appreciate the truly great power of words and the moral hazards that can arise from their misuse. Parents select names and nicknames (words) for their children without acknowledging that they are defining and/or describing who and/or what their child will be for their entire life.

King Solomon teaches in Proverbs 18:21 that *"Death and life are in the power of the tongue, and those who love it will eat its fruits."* (Bible Hub n.d.) In other words, the tongue has the power to determine death and life. Words which are spoken, words which are written can decide whether or not one lives or dies. All of this power lies in words, yet as parents, we bring children into this world and give little or no meaningful contemplation about the name we will bequeath our children. Many of us do a further disservice to our children when we give little or no thought to the words we use when speaking to or expressing ourselves to our children.

Mufasa and Sarabi obviously understood that the name that they assigned to their son was one of the many essential steps to raising a child of purpose. They didn't just give their child any name. They named their son Simba, the Swahili word that means 'lion.'

While it is true that Simba was biologically a lion, the way that he was raised and the lessons that he was taught reflect parents who anticipated that their son would also have the heart and soul of the king of the Pride Land. Simba was strong, courageous, powerful, regal, dignified, authoritarian, ethical, wise, and

It's A Jungle Out There

ferocious, just to name a few of his many attributes. He was those things not because of his feline DNA, but because of his parents' purposeful design to call him what they expected him to become and what the Pride Land needed him to be.

Consider the fate of history today if the names parents chose for their children were not reflective of the virtue, activities, nature, character, and purpose of the child's life. Instead of Jesus Christ, what might have become of the Christian faith if Mary and Joseph had chosen to name their son Midnight Chardonnay? (Tahir 2013) Imagine the effect on civil disobedience worldwide if Mohandas Karamchand Gandhi's parents decided to refer to him as Number 16 Bus Shelter. (Tahir 2013) Envision the state of human and women's rights today, should Jane Adams' parents have elected to call her Talula Does The Hula From Hawaii. (Tahir 2013)

How many people do you believe would subscribe to a faith that had a leader who could not only turn water into wine but was named after a type of wine, Midnight Chardonnay? How effective do you think the people of India would have been in liberating themselves non-violently from the tyranny of British rule if the parents of the movement's leader had named him Number 16 Bus Shelter? Would the American Civil Liberties Union or the National Association for the Advancement of Colored People exist if the founding organizers were required to support Talula Does The Hula From Hawaii?

Nathaniel A. Turner, J.D., MALS

I realize that the names used above seem over the top, but they are actual names of children and symbolic of the naming choices of many parents today. (BabyCenter, L.L.C., 2012)

What does Midnight Chardonnay mean, and what purpose is intended for his life? What design does a parent have for their child's life when they are named after a place typically associated with graffiti and diesel exhaust, Number 16 Bus Shelter? What virtue is implied when a girl is called Talula Does The Hula From Hawaii?

Would anyone be surprised if Midnight Chardonnay grows up to be an alcoholic? Should anyone be shocked if Number 16 Bus Shelter has low self-esteem and is the favorite victim of school bullies? Would anyone be flabbergasted if Talula Does The Hula's name is heard over a loudspeaker in an adult male establishment, "coming to the stage next, gentlemen put your hands together for Ta–lu–la Does The Hu-la"?

The odds are that parents – when we ascribe these unusual names to our children – are making life, which is already challenging on its own, just that much more difficult. This is not solely my opinion, either. Research has shown that names can be the catalyst for problems like lower educational expectations, inferior standardized test scores, lifelong faulty first

It's A Jungle Out There

impressions, low self-esteem, and the eventual imposition of socioeconomic hardships.

Lower Educational Expectations

In December 2003, the University of Florida Professor David N. Figlio published a paper titled "Names, Expectations and Black Children's Achievement." (Figlio, Names, Expectations and Black Children's Achievement 2003)   Dr. Figlio hypothesized that those responsible for educating children expected less of African-American children when they had racially-identifiable names. Dr. Figlio's study found that while African-American children with racially-identifiable names stayed in school longer, their standardized test scores and mathematics scores were lower than African-American children with less racially-identifiable names.

In Dr. Figlio's own words:

> Moreover, all available measures of grading standards and expectations suggests that, within a family, Black children with racially identifiable names are treated differently in school than are those with more homogenized names—conditional on observed test performance, they receive higher grades, but at the same time are more likely to be labeled as learning disabled and less likely to be considered gifted than are their siblings. These results are consistent with the notion that teachers and school

administrators may subconsciously expect less of Black students with racially-identifiable names, and these expectations may possibly become a self-fulfilling prophecy.

According to Dr. Figlio, a name, one impulsive word, can be the reason an educator would expect less of a student and subsequently work against a child's best academic interest. Dr. Carolyn Dweck, the renowned researcher in the field of motivation and a Stanford University professor, provides insight into how and why those accepting the call to educate our children could expect less and work against our children just because of their name. Dr. Dweck, the author of *Mindset*, has found that where there is a fixed mindset, a belief that intelligence and/or ability is fixed, people will no longer attempt to improve and/or grow. (Dweck 2007)

In the case of the African-American student with the racially-identifiable name, if the teacher, the adult charged with cultivating and molding our future, believes the student's intelligence and ability to learn is fixed because of a racially-identifiable name, the teacher will undoubtedly teach to that lowered expectation. When an adult cannot rise above a name to give another human being the absolute best that their profession demands, what would we expect the child taught by that fixed mindset person to think of themselves? The child, more often than not, will believe themselves incapable of excelling academically. Perhaps this is a factor

It's A Jungle Out There

in the crisis that is the American educational system where, according to the Alliance for Excellent Education, "every year, more than 1 million students—that's 7,000 every school day—do not graduate from high school on time". (Alliance For Excellent Education 2011)

It is interesting to note that in the case of Asian students with racially-identifiable names, the opposite of the situation regarding the African-American student is constant. In the case of Asian students, Dr. Figlio observed in his 2004 paper, "Names, Expectations and the Black-White Test Score Gap," that the racially-identifiable Asian name was associated with success. (Figlio, Names, Expectations And The Black-White Test Score Gap 2005) In other words, the teacher's expectations of the Asian students were higher, and the accompanying examination scores were higher as well. The Asian students were bolstered by a "growth mindset," which, according to Dr. Dweck, is a belief that our ability to learn, change, and develop needed skills is infinite.

A name, a couple of simple words, determines teachers' perceptions, attitudes, and expectations of Asian students. A person's name, one or more words, made it possible for the Asian students to be educated in an environment that prepared them for success, leaving the Asian student better equipped to handle the inevitable challenges of school and of life.

Nathaniel A. Turner, J.D., MALS

Economic Hardship

In September 2004, Dr. Marianne Bertrand and Dr. Sendhil Mullainathan asked the question, "Are Emily and Greg More Employable than Lakisha and Jamal?" (Bertrand and Mullainathan 2003) The University of Chicago professor and MIT professor conducted a study to determine whether job applicants with racially-identifiable African-American names were considered for employment at the same rate as "White-sounding" names. Drs. Bertrand and Mullainathan responded to 1,300 job ads in The Boston Globe and Chicago Tribune using the content of 500 real resumes off online job boards.

The study found that applicants with racially-identifiable African-American names were 50% less likely to receive calls for interviews than the applicants with "White-sounding" names. Racially-identifiable African-American names received a request for an interview 6.7% of the time. "White-sounding" names received a request for an interview 10% of the time. Even when coupling the racially-identifiable African-American name with a superior resume including education, experience, and skills, the African-American applicant only received a call for an interview 9% of the time as opposed to the 30% callback for the applicant with the "White-sounding" name. In real-world terminology, that is nine interviews for every 100 African-American applicants and 30 interviews for every 100 white applicants.

It's A Jungle Out There

Once again, one name, a couple of simple words, might make one 333% more likely to receive a call for an interview. Dr. Bertrand and Dr. Mullainathan's study seems to infer something eerily similar to Dr. Figlio's study. Segments of our population, such as teachers, school administrators, and employers, often assume intelligence, ability, and employability from a name. As is the case for racially-identifiable African-American names, conscious or unconscious biases of educators and employers can be as much a factor in a person's opportunity to succeed as the person's own intellect, education, ability, experience, and skills.

Let me be clear, I am not suggesting that a family should pick a traditional "Anglo-Saxon" or "Asian" name for their child, nor do I mean to suggest that life for children with "Anglo-Saxon" or "Asian" names is guaranteed to be more comfortable because it brings with it better grades, higher standardized test scores and uncomplicated employability. Moreover, neither am I suggesting that a family should deny its desire to name a child something culturally relevant, inspired by religion or merely unique.

What I would suggest is that like Mufasa and Sarabi, you give some real consideration to whatever name you eventually choose for your child and understand the potential socioeconomic issues involved in the selection of a name. I would further suggest that like Mufasa

Nathaniel A. Turner, J.D., MALS

and Sarabi, you give your child a name that personifies positivity and virtue, and if possible that you select a name that your child can strive to live up to regarding its meaning.

For those parents who are determined that a "really unique" name is the only viable option, the research and facts show that you must be exceptionally engaged, positive, reassuring, involved, and supportive in your child's life. You must convince your child in ways that other parents will not have to do that not only is their name "exceptional," but that their life is intended to be extraordinary, as well. Your parental challenge will be more taxing as you will have to assure your child that their name is life-affirming and that it has a predictive purpose for their life.

It may feel unfair, but those of us who choose to give our children a "distinctive" name must be prepared to parent incomparably because, as of this moment, the world we live still has its challenges when it comes to race and gender perceptions. Hopefully, one day, we will live in a world where racially-identifiable and "distinctive" names are not synonymous with defective prejudgments and diminished expectations.

Until that time comes, parents should think long and hard about the names we choose and the words we use when referring to our children, always remembering, like Simba's parents, that the names we select and the terms we use can

It's A Jungle Out There

speak life or death into existence for our children and maybe our land.

Rule No. 8: Your Child is a Narcissist.

I suspect that this rule is going to be exceptionally hard for some to accept. So before I go any further, I am going to make this disclaimer: I am not a doctor or psychologist, so when I use the word *narcissist*, I do so as a layperson. Now that the lawyers and mental health authorities or, as I prefer to reference them, the Adult Professional Narcissists have been satisfied, I want you to know that your little bundle of joy is on their way (if they haven't already arrived at the unavoidable destination) to becoming a full-fledged narcissist.

Dictionary.com defines *narcissism* as "an inordinate fascination with oneself; excessive self-love; vanity. Synonyms: self-centeredness, smugness, egocentrism". Now, if your little bundle of joy is still a baby, you can just watch the young narcissist in action to fully grasp the definition. If they are no longer babies, you'll have to rely as I do on memory or wait for about five minutes before they make some egotistical statement or do something selfish to remind you of who they are in reality.

In case you are unfamiliar with the word narcissist, *'narcissist'* has its origin in Greek mythology. Narcissus was a young man who, while looking into a pool of water, saw his own image and fell in love with himself. He could not be satisfied with the appearance of anyone other than himself. The result was that he died and

It's A Jungle Out There

was transformed into a flower, which is now named after him. We now consider those who are self-indulged to be a narcissist.

Sigmund Freud theorized that all human beings experience a period of life as narcissists. Professor Freud hypothesized that the first state of narcissistic behavior occurs at birth. He termed this early period of narcissistic behavior "primary narcissism."

Primary narcissism was identified as the "auto-erotic" stage of self-love that babies go through in their first year of life. This is the period were babies are solely focused on themselves and their own needs. (Markotic 201)

As a layperson, I didn't know that this period was called "primary narcissism," but I do remember a time when my son seemed capable only of thinking about himself. I called this time of his life the "Revocation of the Emancipation Proclamation" period. During the period from birth through the first few months of his life, I was convinced that my son hadn't realized that slavery had been abolished.

I remember asking myself, "Is this all there once a baby is birthed? He eats, naps, drinks, pees, defecates, and starts the process all over again." I thought, "what a selfish brat he is turning out to be. All this stinking kid does is think about himself." I really wondered if slavery had been reestablished. Not knowing what it meant to be

Nathaniel A. Turner, J.D., MALS

a father, the 24/7 attentiveness seemed utterly ridiculous.

My son cried, and someone had to prepare his food. My son cried, and someone had to change his diaper. My son cried, and someone had to wake up to hold him. My son cried, and someone had to burp him. My son cried, and someone had to take him for a car ride. My son cried, and someone had to bathe him. My son cried, and someone had to do something for him. It was an exhausting, depressing, and dissatisfying time, especially for anyone designated as the "someone."

One day, a day when I had an exceptionally challenging day at work, my son poked me. When I looked back at my wife thinking she had been the one to poke me and to ask her why she was bothering me, she quickly exclaimed: "it's not me; it's your son." I turned to look at my son, he smiled and then laughed. It was as if he knew his dad needed him to think about somebody other than himself for once. It felt like he was telling me everything was going to be okay. For the first time, my little bundle of narcissism saw fit to do something other than love himself.

Now my good fortune where my son thought of someone other than himself lasted only for that moment, but it was a sign that he had the potential to see the world as something more than a place that should satisfy all of his whims and desires. I have come to understand that my

It's A Jungle Out There

experiences with my son during his infant period were ordinary. Children, especially newborns, demand constant attention. What I thought was modern-day indentured servitude was merely his biological process of survival, a natural process of survival that is found in every child, even those children like Simba who are of royal birth.

Narcissism, I learned, was acceptable during infancy but not beyond. Unchecked narcissism becomes something ugly, dangerous, and unacceptable to society. My only son, like Mufasa's son, would remain a narcissist and be a danger to himself and the broader community unless he was taught that he was not the only one on earth with bona fide needs.

Convincing a child that others are of equal importance is no easy task. Even Mufasa's attempt to socialize his son so that he would think about someone other than himself was initially rebuffed. Instead, Simba's state of mind was to remain a narcissist. Only moments after his father had painstakingly explained to him that there was more to being king than getting your way all the time, that everything exists in a delicate balance and that we are all connected in the "Great Circle of Life," Simba quickly dismissed his father's advice for his own self-satisfaction.

Not only does Simba dismiss Mufasa's advice with his behavior, but he sings a song about it:

Nathaniel A. Turner, J.D., MALS

> I'm gonna be a mighty king, so enemies beware
> I'm gonna be the main event like no king was before
> I'm brushing up on looking down, I'm working on my roar
> Oh, I just can't wait to be king!
> No one saying 'do this,' no one saying 'be there.'
> No one saying 'stop that,' no one saying 'see here.'
> Free to run around all day, free to do it all my way!
> Everybody look left, everybody look right
> Everywhere you look, I'm standing in the spotlight (John and Rice 1994)

The words Simba sings and his subsequent actions revealed traits that are so commonly found in narcissists – unremitting talk about themselves, indifference towards others, embellishment of their abilities, and more. A primary task of parents today is to temper our children's narcissistic tendencies and ideology.

We have our hands full as we have raised a generation where far too many of our children are growing up and have grown up feeling entitled. We have raised children who feel entitled to a trophy just because. We have convinced children that everyone should feel good even if they didn't do anything other than put on a uniform. In school children believe they are entitled to a grade of no less than a "C" because, well, everyone should receive a passing

It's A Jungle Out There

grade even if the work was only worth an "F". When our children reach so-called life landmarks, we have influenced them to believe that they are entitled to something extraordinary when they turn sixteen, eighteen and graduate from high school because, well, everyone is exceptional even if they never did anything special or never did anything for anyone other than themselves. Children become adults who feel entitled to a life of luxury because, well, they possess the same last name and dwelt in the home of the people who alone worked painstakingly, sweating profusely and shedding blood and tears to create a life their children consider a birthright.

Today's parents have made our job of parenting more difficult. We are responsible for many of society's ills. We have been so focused on wanting to give our children the best that we have unintentionally raised children who deserve little but feel entitled to everything.

Today's children shoot others when they are teased. Today's children rape when others are intoxicated and unwilling participants. Today's children take their own lives when they feel less important than all the other self-important children.

There could be no better time for us to start raising our little bundles of joy to know that little bundles of joy cannot do whatever they want and that there is more to being a little bundle of joy than getting your way all the time.

Nathaniel A. Turner, J.D., MALS

The time is now for parents to raise children who understand that if the world is to survive, everything has to exist together with a delicate self-sacrificing balance.

Rule No. 9: Train Your Child to be a Great Citizen.

In Rule No. 8, I referenced the edict Mufasa shared with Simba. Mufasa's pronouncement was something that our society, which is growing increasingly uncivil, needs more parents to embrace and subsequently train their children to adopt.

In case you have been living in another country or on another planet – Americans are becoming increasingly discourteous. From the classroom to the meeting room and from the boardroom to the courtroom, Americans continue to display a lack of decorum that would undoubtedly topple any country, this great nation included.

Incivility in America is rampant and is quickly becoming the norm rather than the exception. In particular, incivility with and among our children is reaching epidemic levels. One need only examine the state of American high schools to see that they have become the training grounds for not only future unscrupulous business leaders and discourteous politicians, but burglars, thieves, kidnappers, extortionists, embezzlers, murders, and rapists, as well.

For most, it has been no secret that American children bear some additional burdens trying to read, write, and count as demonstrated by the most recent Program for International Student Assessment (PISA) rankings. Among the 34

Nathaniel A. Turner, J.D., MALS

Organization for Economic Co-operation and Development (OECD) countries, the United States ranks 14th in reading, 17th in science and 25th in mathematics. (Walker 2010) This is a deplorable ranking for a nation that prides itself and references itself as "The Leader of the Free World."

As a side note, is a nation that is ranked 14th in reading, 17th in science and 25th in mathematics actually the "Leader" of anything? This is perhaps a question we should explore at a later time.

For now, let's focus on America's incivility problem – a problem that is less commonly known than the poor academic standings highlighted by PISA, and a dilemma that has been in some ways kept secret or gone underappreciated by the American public. America is not only inadequate in its educational preparation, but we are doing an equally poor job preparing our children to be citizens of their own country. Not to mention, we are doing a lackluster job of training them to be "leading citizens of the free world."

In 2011, the U.S. Department of Health and Human Services, in conjunction with its subsidiary, the Centers for Disease Control and Prevention, conducted a survey on youth risk behavior. The findings are documented in the "Youth Risk Behavior Surveillance" (U.S. Department of Health and Human Services 2012) study, which was published on June 8,

It's A Jungle Out There

2012, in the *Morbidity and Mortality Weekly Report*. The 162-page report describes some startling facts about the increasing levels of incivility among America's youth:

- 20.1% of students had been bullied on school property (U.S. Department of Health and Human Services 2012)
- 5.1% of students had carried a gun; the prevalence of having possessed a firearm was higher among males (8.6%) than females (1.4%) (U.S. Department of Health and Human Services 2012)
- 16.6% of students had carried a weapon (e.g., a gun, knife, or club); the prevalence of having carried a weapon was higher among male (25.9%) than female (6.8%) students (U.S. Department of Health and Human Services 2012)
- 7.4% of students had been threatened or injured with a weapon (e.g., a gun, knife, or club) on school property one or more times (U.S. Department of Health and Human Services 2012)
- 32.8% of students had been in a physical fight one or more times (U.S. Department of Health and Human Services 2012)
- 16.2% of students had been electronically bullied, including being bullied through e-mail, chat rooms, instant messaging, websites, or texting; the prevalence of having been electronically bullied was higher among female (22.1%) than male (10.8%) students (U.S. Department of Health and Human Services 2012)

- 5.9% of students had not gone to school on at least one day because they felt they would be unsafe at school or on their way to or from school (U.S. Department of Health and Human Services 2012)
- 26.1% of students had had their property (e.g., car, clothing or books) stolen or deliberately damaged on school property one or more times (U.S. Department of Health and Human Services 2012)
- 9.4% of students nationwide had been hit, slapped or physically hurt on purpose by their boyfriend or girlfriend (i.e., dating violence) (U.S. Department of Health and Human Services 2012)
- 8.0% of students had been physically forced to have sexual intercourse when they did not want to; the prevalence of having been forced to have sexual intercourse was higher among female (11.8%) than male (4.5%) students (U.S. Department of Health and Human Services 2012)
- 7.8% of students had attempted suicide one or more times (U.S. Department of Health and Human Services 2012)

The findings of the survey illustrate that American children, like young Simba, fail to recognize and accept the prerequisites of citizenship. It would appear from the results above that a few things are unquestionably certain.

It's A Jungle Out There

Our children have not been adequately instructed about the true meaning of citizenship. Also, those assigned to training our future "Leaders of the Free World" have done an utterly inadequate job. The behavior of our children suggests a grave misunderstanding about the roles of citizens and the importance of adhering to the requirements of being a citizen.

Our children must know and understand that citizenship cannot be reduced to only living in the country and enjoying the legal and social rights of the nation. As Mufasa explains to Simba, a citizen not only has the right to enjoy the legal and social benefits of society, but a citizen also shoulders the legal and moral obligation to conduct themselves in a fashion that at the very least sustains the *status quo*, even if it does not actually improve upon the society.

Fortunately for Simba, he had a father who understood the meaning and role of a citizen. One particular conversation between Mufasa and Simba details what is required of anyone, including the King, to maintain Pride Land's societal structure. Not only were the words Mufasa spoke to Simba valuable instructions, but his words are equally applicable and beneficial to those responsible for maintaining and continuing America's distinction as "Leader of the Free World."

I refer to Mufasa's instructions to Simba as a three-part Societal Maintenance Plan – a plan that is capable of helping to raise and improve citizenship standards in a country like America that, by all appearance, seems to be experiencing a rapid decline in civility.

The first provision of the Societal Maintenance Plan is found in the following exchange between Mufasa and Simba:

> Simba: But I thought a king can do whatever he wants.
> Mufasa: There's more to being a king than getting your way all the time.
> Simba: There's more?
> Mufasa: [chuckling] Simba.

The dialogue above is the first insight that being a citizen of a country or, in the case of Simba, the heir apparent to a kingdom comes with absolute requirements. Mufasa is clear that citizens get to enjoy their rights and privileges, but they are no less responsible for respecting and upholding the rights and privileges of all others.

The second provision of Mufasa's three-part Societal Maintenance Plan is revealed when Mufasa shares these words with Simba:

> Mufasa: Everything you see exists together in a delicate balance. As king, you need to understand that balance and respect all the creatures, from the crawling ant to the leaping antelope.

It's A Jungle Out There

Mufasa explains to Simba that the greatness of the Pride Land lies in its ability to ensure that everything coexists harmoniously. In Pride Land, every creature understands and works to fulfill their societal responsibility.

Mufasa conveys to his son that this joint partnership is a fragile relationship and would not work without the equal and complementary participation of all parties. Furthermore, Mufasa's words prescribe that the joint collaboration will fail if the citizens don't understand how the kingdom was intended to function. If the members of the society don't appreciate the frailty of personal relationships and show high regard for all living creatures (the citizens), Pride Land – like America – will no longer be the place the light touches.

The third and final provision of Mufasa's three-part Societal Maintenance Plan is that everyone must understand that while we may be different, we all share evenly critical roles in the survival of our society.

> Simba: But, Dad, don't we eat the antelope?
> Mufasa: Yes, Simba, but let me explain. When we die, our bodies become the grass, and the antelope eat the grass. And so we are all connected in the Great Circle of Life.

Nathaniel A. Turner, J.D., MALS

Mufasa's explanation above details the interdependence that exists among all creatures. There is no lion without antelope for them to eat. Similarly, there is no antelope to eat without the death of the lion, which fertilizes the grass that the antelope eats. The symbiotic relationship that holds the Pride Land together, making it a place that the "Light" touches, is similar to the symbiotic relationship that sustains all great nations.

America cannot exist in the form we have come to expect if we don't sustain, restore, and nurture those symbiotic relationships that once distinguished us as true "Leaders of the Free World." America's ability to produce and train children who understand and embrace their role and responsibility as not only U.S. citizens but leading citizens of "the Free World" is the first step towards restoring and improving civility. America cannot exist if it is inhabited by a nation of entitled, uncivil citizens.

To do anything other than follow Mufasa's Societal Maintenance Plan may doom our nation to become a land like the Pride Land when it was ruled by Scar - a territory that was barren, desolate, under toxic leadership and overrun by hyenas; an area so lacking incivility that those with good manners despised calling it their home.

Rule No. 10: Failure is Not a Child's Best Way to Learn

I have often heard it quoted that failure should be our teacher. Implicit in this philosophy is that through failure – or maybe more accurately trial and error – we learn more about ourselves than at any other time. Through this failing to succeed methodology, we not only learn about ourselves, but if we are fortunate enough, we finally accomplish our goals and/or master the task at hand.

Like most, I have experienced the application of this philosophy firsthand. While I freely admit that there were times in my life that figuring out how to do something on my own after having failed at it many times gave me a great sense of accomplishment, I am unconvinced that this philosophy is always the best way to approach learning or to achieve the intended outcome.

Sadly, some believe *"failure should always be our teacher"* and apply this philosophy as a blanket rule to cover all of life's situations. In particular, as it relates to raising children, I believe this philosophy and methodology of teaching is often misapplied in far too many cases. The following two scenarios illustrate my viewpoint.

The Soldier

Imagine a young man who graduates from high school and enlists in the Army. On the same day that the young man joins, he is whisked around the world to Afghanistan. Once the young soldier lands, he is ordered by his superior officer to go out into a street that is believed to be a minefield of Improvised Explosive Devices (IEDs).

Without any instruction, training, or practice, the soldier will almost certainly set off one of the IEDs. The result is that the soldier will likely blow himself up and die or at the very least, suffer some catastrophic injury. The soldier's death or extreme impairment will be a lesson from which he can never fully recuperate. The soldier's death or physical wounds will be an emotional and financial hardship from which his family will have to attempt to recover.

Although this scenario is purely fictional, I imagine the deceased or disabled soldier and his surviving or caretaking family would vehemently disagree with the philosophy *"failure should be our teacher."*

The Driver

Picture a Monday morning rush hour drive. The roads are congested. There are irritated drivers in every lane. The traffic is 'bump and go.' Drivers experiencing road rage are in abundance. Half the drivers have only one hand on the wheel while they consume their breakfast with the other hand. The other half of drivers have only one hand on the steering wheel while they text or talk on the phone.

It's A Jungle Out There

Now envision that these drivers are our children driving off to high school each morning. See in your mind's eye what the fate of America's roads and highways might be if 'failure' was allowed to be our children's driving teacher.

Pretend that instead of learning to drive from a driver's education program, our youngest, most ill-equipped drivers learned exclusively through failure. The motto might as well be "Give the kids the keys and let them play bumper cars." This ill-fated scenario is just one of many examples where the application of the *"failure should be our teacher"* philosophy is a recipe for massive disaster, just as it was for our soldier.

To further drive home, the point about the potential chaos such a philosophy has as it is applied to children, consider the nation's teenage driving statistics. As things currently stand, even with mandatory driver's education and other restrictions, our newest, least prepared drivers – teen drivers – are the statistically worst drivers on the roads. The comparison between teenage drivers and adult drivers is not even close.

The CDC reports that teen driving, even with driver's education and additional mandates, is an enormous problem. The "CDC's Teen Drivers: Fact Sheet" gives some insight into how much worse the roads could be if 'failure' were always the best teacher.

Nathaniel A. Turner, J.D., MALS

> Motor vehicle crashes are the leading cause of death for U.S. teens. In 2017, six teens ages 16 to 19 died every day from motor vehicle injuries. Per mile drove, teen drivers ages 16 to 19 are three times more likely than drivers aged 20 and older to be in a fatal crash... (Centers for Disease Control and Prevention 2019)

> In 2017, about 2,364 teens in the United States aged 16 to19 were killed, and almost 300,000 were treated and released from emergency departments for injuries suffered in motor vehicle crashes. Young people ages 15 to 19 represent only 6.5% of the U.S. population. However, they account for 8% ($13.1 billion) of the total costs of motor vehicle injuries. (Centers for Disease Control and Prevention 2019)

Hopefully, the scenarios of the untrained soldier and the IEDs and teenage drivers rushing off to high school give you some pause in believing and professing *"failure as the best teacher."* I hope you would agree with me considering the two scenarios that the outcomes associated with the application of the "failure as the best teacher" philosophy can have dire consequences.

If you wonder what optional methods of learning are available, Mufasa fortuitously illustrates an alternative way to train our children, which is more efficient and expeditious. It is an option that would minimize the mass calamity, property

It's A Jungle Out There

damage, and destruction caused in the scenarios above that both illustrate the flaws in the "failure should be our teacher" philosophy.

Pouncing Lesson

In the early part of *The Lion King*, Mufasa notices Simba attempting to catch a grasshopper. Simba's attempts to pounce on the grasshopper are unsuccessful. Upon seeing his son's struggle, Mufasa offers Simba his assistance:

> Mufasa: What are you doing, Son?
> Simba: Pouncing.
> Mufasa: Let a pro show you how it's done.

Mufasa's words "let a pro show you how it's done" offer a methodology for training children that is inherently far superior to "*failure as a teacher.*" Mufasa was a professional, an expert at pouncing. Rather than have his son waste time and energy failing until he succeeded, Mufasa decided to instruct his son in the art of pouncing. Not only did Mufasa provide instructions for his son, but he did so as soon as he noticed the difficulties his son was having.

Imagine the direction the story could have taken, and the pending doom Pride Land might have suffered if Mufasa did not stop at that precise moment to teach his son how to pounce. Mufasa would meet his death shortly after that. Had he not stopped to teach Simba this valuable lesson precisely when he did, one can surmise

Nathaniel A. Turner, J.D., MALS

that Simba would not have known how to pounce or how to do so proficiently.

Knowing how to pounce was an essential element of survival for Simba. The pouncing lesson was instruction in not only how to secure food but in self-defense. Without the tutorial, it is highly unlikely that Simba would have survived in the jungle with Timon and Pumbaa or been able to return to the Pride Land and defeat his uncle Scar.

Mufasa's decision to instruct Simba leaves me wondering how much better our children might be if instead of watching them fail until they succeed or – and this is more likely – fail until they quit, we commit like Mufasa to providing early expert instruction. What if we followed Mufasa's example and treated our children like our apprentices rather than an experiment on the value and probability of failure? What if we thought the future of our kingdom, as was in Mufasa's illustration or in our case the future of our country, was dependent on the preparation of our children? Might we interrupt our morning report (business meeting), stop whatever we are doing dead in our tracks, to instruct our child on elements that would make it possible for them to survive and prosper individually, and that would assist with the collective survival of our land?

Literacy

It's A Jungle Out There

I contend that as a nation, we too often choose to watch our children flounder unsuccessfully when we would be better served by implementing Mufasa's methods of giving on the spot hands-on instruction. Such is the case with America's despicable literacy rates. For too long, it appears America has applied the philosophy "failure is the best teacher" to reading and reading proficiency. Consider some facts about Literacy as reported by DoSomething.org: (DoSomething.org 2015)

1. Two-thirds of students who cannot read proficiently by the end of fourth grade will end up in jail or on welfare. Over 70 percent of America's inmates cannot read above a fourth-grade level.

2. One in four children in America grows up without learning how to read.

3. As of 2011, America was the only free-market OECD country where the current generation was less educated than the previous one.

4. Literacy is a learned skill. Illiteracy is passed down from parents who can neither read nor write.

5. Nearly 85 percent of the juveniles who face trial in the juvenile court system are functionally illiterate, proving that there is a close relationship between illiteracy and crime. More than 60 percent of all inmates

are functionally illiterate.

6. Fifty-three percent of fourth-graders admitted to reading recreationally "almost every day," while only 20 percent of eighth-graders could say the same. (2009 study)

7. Seventy-five percent of Americans who receive food stamps perform at the two lowest levels of literacy, and 90% of high school dropouts are on welfare.

8. Teenage girls ages 16 to 19 who live at or below the poverty level and have below-average literacy skills are six times more likely to have children out of wedlock than the girls their age who can read proficiently.

9. Reports show that low literacy directly costs the healthcare industry over $70 million every year.

Worse than having an abundance of illiterate children is having illiterate children reside in a nation with an excess of Masters, Ph.Ds., Ed.Ds., M.Ds., and J.Ds. A country that is made up of professionals who are if nothing more skilled at reading and who are either unwilling or unable to help children academically is inexcusable. This is more than an inconvenient truth; it is an appalling reality.

It's A Jungle Out There

The dictum *"Failure as the best teacher"* is not working as it relates to teaching America's children to read and advance our society. Our children, as evidenced by the statistics made available by DoSomething.org, are failing miserably like Simba trying to pounce on the grasshopper. If we don't change our way of thinking, we will not have a similar fairy-tale happy ending.

Literacy in America can only change when America's parents stop considering failure to be the best teacher of America's children. America needs more Mufasas to step in and step up to provide professional aid. America needs immediate expert assistance made available from all those capable experts who are not seeking solely to help the cause so that they may make a name for themselves. Immediate expert assistance is necessary from all those accomplished professionals who are not of the mindset that providing professional quality aid deprives children of knowing the benefits of hard work and pulling themselves up by their own bootstraps.

America also needs more Zazus to be willing to make the necessary sacrifices to ensure that the learning process is successful. In the same way that Zazu was prepared to be humiliated so that Simba could learn to pounce expeditiously and efficiently, America needs those dignified highly-ranking advisors who have previously consciously or unconsciously subscribed to *"failure as the best teacher"* to be willing to do

Nathaniel A. Turner, J.D., MALS

whatever is necessary to best prepare the children of our nation. Be it through more significant exposure to teachers, NEA, politicians, prisons, governmental agencies, or parents, American children should all be allowed to receive expert guidance from whomever and whenever as soon as possible and for as long as possible.

Expert guidance is not an evil crutch that provides an unfair advantage. Professional assistance expedites merely the learning process of pulling oneself up by one's own bootstraps. I encourage America to seek and offer the same instruction for all of its children.

I'm not advocating that adults do the work for children. I'm advocating that every child receive the expert instruction that will expedite the learning process, making it more likely that all children will achieve the educational goals and objectives, which in truth will sustain our nation.

Mufasa did not pounce on Zazu for Simba, he merely provided expert instruction until Simba learned to pounce himself successfully. Thanks to Mufasa's adept guidance and Zazu's "take one for the team" attitude, Simba was not forced to spend precious time and countless hours failing until he hopefully succeeded or, worse, just quit trying.

We already know that failure is always highly probable where there is no experience and non-

It's A Jungle Out There

existent or ineffective training. Why, then, the incessant need to continue testing something that has already been proven time and again to be accurate? If, as a nation, we intend to keep challenging already resolved truths, we might as well begin investigating whether the world is round or flat.

References

Alliance For Excellent Education. 2011. "The High Cost of High School Dropouts: What the Nation Pays for Inadequate High Schools." *Issue Brief* 6.

American Academy of Child and Adolescent Psychiatry. 2017. *Home Alone Children.* October. Accessed 2012. https://www.aacap.org/AACAP/Families_and_Youth/Facts_for_Families/FFF-Guide/Home-Alone-Children-046.aspx.

American Humane. 2018. *Child Abuse and Neglect Statistics.* Accessed 2012. http://www.americanhumane.org/children/stop-child-abuse/fact-sheets/child-abuse-and-neglect-statistics.html.

Answers.com. 2012. *What percentage of eligible Americans vote?* Accessed 2012. http://qa.answers.com/Q/What_percentage_of_eligible_Americans_vote.

Association for Behavioral and Cognitive Therapies. n.d. "Injury Prevention In Preschool Children." *http://www.abct.org/Information/?m=mInformation&fa=fs_INJURY_PREVENTION.* Accessed 2012. http://www.abct.org/docs/factsheets/INJURY_PREVENTION.pdf.

BabyCenter, L.L.C.. 2012. *Unusual and Surprising Baby Names.* Accessed 2012. https://www.babycenter.com/0_unusual-and-surprising-baby-names_10388919.bc.

It's A Jungle Out There

Bertrand, Marianne, and Sendhil Mullainathan. 2003. "Are Emily and Greg More Employable Than Lakisha and Jamal? A Field Experiment on Labor Market Discrimination." *National Bureau of Economic Research* 40.

Bible Hub. n.d. *Proverbs 18:21.* Accessed 2012. http://biblehub.com/proverbs/18-21.htm.

Bronson, Po. 2008. *Learning to Lie.* February 10. Accessed 2012. http://nymag.com/news/features/43893/index2.html.

Centers for Disease Control and Prevention. 2019. *Motor Vehicle Safety.* October 30. Accessed November 13, 2019. https://www.cdc.gov/motorvehiclesafety/teen_drivers/teendrivers_factsheet.html.

Child Trends Databank. 2015. *Children in Poverty.* December. Accessed 2012. https://www.childtrends.org/files/child_trends-2009_04_07_rb_childreninpoverty.pdf.

Children's Bureau. 2012. "Child Maltreatment." *U.S. Department of Health and Human Services, Administration for Children and Families, Administration on Children, Youth and Families, Children's Bureau* 251. Accessed 2012. http://www.childhelp.org/pages/statistics.

DoSomething.org. 2015. *11 Facts About Literacy in America.* February 24. Accessed November 13, 2019. https://www.dosomething.org/us/facts/11-facts-about-literacy-america.

Dweck, Carol S., 2007. *Mindset: The New Psychology of Success.* New York: Ballantine Books.

Figlio, David N., 2003. *Names, Expectations and Black Children's Achievement.* Gainsville: University of Florida and NBER.

Figlio, David N., 2005. "Names, Expectations And The Black-White Test Score Gap." *National Bureau of Economic Research* 32.

Guang Guo, Elizabeth Stearns. 2002. "The Social Influences on the Realization of Genetic Potential for Intellectual Development." *Oxford Academic*, March 1: 881-910.

John, Elton, and Tim Rice. 1994. *I Just Can't Wait to Be King.* Cond. Walt Disney Music Company. Comp. Walt Disney Music Company.

Markotic, Lorraine. 201. "There Where Primary Narcissism Was, I Must Become: The Inception of the Ego in Andreas-Salomé, Lacan, and Kristeva." *JSTOR* 24.

National Fatherhood Initiative. 2012. *Father Absence + Involvement | Statistics.* Accessed 2012. https://www.fatherhood.org/fatherhood-data-statistics.

NPR: All Things Considered. 2009. *Parenting Tips: Praise Can Be Bad; Lying Is Normal.* August 27. Accessed 2012. https://www.npr.org/templates/story/story.php?storyId=112292248.

Quinlan, Robert J., 2003. "Father Absence, Parental Care, and Female Reproductive Development." *Evolution and Human Behavior* 15.

Tahir, Tariq. 2013. *New Zealand reveals new list of banned names for babies – including Lucifer and 4Real.* May 1. Accessed 2013. https://metro.co.uk/2013/05/01/new-zealand-reveals-new-list-of-banned-names-for-babies-3709255/.

The Liz Library. 2012. *The Effects of Pregnancy.* Accessed 2012. http://www.thelizlibrary.org/site-index/site-index-

It's A Jungle Out There

frame.html#soulhttp://www.thelizlibrary.org/liz/004.htm.

Thompson, Derek. 2010. "80 Percent of Americans Don't Trust the Government. Here's Why." *The Atlantic.* April 19. Accessed 2012. https://www.theatlantic.com/business/archive/2010/04/80-percent-of-americans-dont-trust-the-government-heres-why/39148/.

U.S. Department of Health & Human Services. 2012. *Child Maltreatment 2011.* December 12. Accessed 2012. https://www.acf.hhs.gov/cb/resource/child-maltreatment-2011.

U.S. Department of Health and Human Services. 2012. "Youth Risk Behavior Surveillance - United States, 2011." *Morbidity and Mortality Weekly Report* 168.

United States Census Bureau. 2011. *Custodial Mothers and Fathers and Their Child Support: 2009.* December. Accessed 2012. https://www.census.gov/prod/2011pubs/p60-240.pdf.

Walker, Tim. 2010. *NEA Today.* December 7. Accessed November 13, 2019. http://neatoday.org/2010/12/07/pisa2009/.

Wolf, Jennifer. 2018. *The Single Parent Statistics Based on Census Data.* May 22. Accessed 2012. https://www.verywellfamily.com/single-parent-census-data-2997668.

Nathaniel A. Turner, J.D., MALS

www.ingramcontent.com/pod-product-compliance
Lightning Source LLC
Chambersburg PA
CBHW050601300426
44112CB00013B/2014